Winning TOEFL

Yuri Yi

Listening Step 3

Step 3

Step 2

Step 1

Winning TOEFL is a three-step series for beginning level students who are preparing for the TOEFL iBT. Each step consists of four books: Listening, Reading, Speaking and Writing. Winning TOEFL will help students be familiar with TOEFL iBT question types and provide opportunities to develop essential test skills through a step-by-step process.

Wit & Wisdom is the professional language publishing company of the **PAGODA** Education Group.

UNIT 1

- tend to
- colony
- specialize
- specialty
- figure out
- artificial
- larva
- efficient
- seismic
- vibration
- compression
- shear
- boundary
- overwhelming
- indeed
- elective
- impact
- meteorite
- peninsula
- extinction
- plateau
- subsequent
- grief
- assign
- sophisticated
- conduct
- captive
- neuroscience
- get absorbed
- passionate
- submit
- chairperson
- prevalent
- superior
- **Triassic period**
- adapt
- coincidence
- habitat
- impact
- emerge
- endangered
- makeup
- intergovernmental
- panel
- spare
- be in the same boat
- frustration
- fire regulation
- petition

- **tend to** ~하는 경향이 있다
  to be inclined to

- **colony** (n) 군집, 집단; 식민지
  a group of the same kind of animals living together

- **specialize** (v) ~을 전문으로 하다
  to concentrate on a particular activity or product

- **specialty** (n) 전문, 전공
  a special skill or characteristic

- **figure out** ~을 이해하다, 알아내다
  to solve; discover; understand

- **artificial** (adj) 인공의, 인위적인
  made by human beings; synthetic; non-natural

- **larva** (n) 유충, 애벌레
  the newly hatched form of an insect (pl. larvae)

- **efficient** (adj) 효율적인, 능률적인
  effective; productive

- **seismic** (adj) 지진의, 지진에 의한
  of or caused by an earthquake

- **vibration** (n) 떨림, 진동
  tremor; trembling

- **compression** (n) 압축
  the process of putting pressure

- **shear** (n) (양의) 털을 깎음; 부러짐, 전단(剪斷)
  the process of moving as if by cutting

- **boundary** (n) 경계(선)
  border; limit

- **overwhelming** (adj) 압도적인, 대응하기 힘든
  overpowering; being affected strongly

- **indeed** (adv) 정말로
  without a doubt; certainly

- **elective** (n) 선택 과목
  a subject which a student can choose to study

- **impact** (n) 충돌, 충격
  collision; crash; smash

- **meteorite** (n) 운석
  a matter that has fallen from outer space to the Earth's surface

- **peninsula** (n) 반도
  a piece of land that sticks out from a larger piece of land and surrounded by water

- **extinction** (n) 멸종
  dying out; abolition; destruction

- **plateau** (n) 고원
  a large area of high and fairly flat land

- **subsequent** (adj) 그 다음의
  following; after; later

- **grief** (n) 비탄, 큰 슬픔
  deep emotional pain; torment

- **assign** (v) (일, 책임 등을) 맡기다
  to place; appoint

- **sophisticated** (adj) 세련된, 정교한
  refined; complicated

- **conduct** (v) 지휘하다
  to lead or guide; control

- **captive** (adj) 억류된
  kept under control; confined

- **neuroscience** (n) 신경 과학
  any of the sciences dealing with the nervous system

- **get absorbed** ~에 몰두하다
  to be wholly involved; be really into something

- **passionate** `adj` 격정적인
  affected by intense feeling; enthusiastic

- **submit** `v` 제출하다
  to propose or hand something in for review or decision

- **chairperson** `n` 의장
  the head of an organization or department

- **prevalent** `adj` 일반적인, 널리 퍼져 있는
  commonly existing; prevailing

- **superior** `adj` 우수한
  of great value; of higher nature

- **Triassic period** 트라이아스기 (중생대를 셋으로 나눈 것 중 첫 번째 기간)
  the geologic time of the first period of Mesozoic Era, before the Jurassic Period

- **adapt** `v` 맞추다
  to become suitable to fit a specific situation

- **coincidence** `n` 우연의 일치
  accident; something happening by chance or luck

- **habitat** `n` 서식지
  the area or environment in which animals or plants live

- **impact** (n) 영향
  influence; effect

- **emerge** (v) 나오다; 드러나다, 알려지다
  to rise; become clear

- **endangered** (adj) 위험에 처한; 멸종될 위기에 이른
  faced with the danger of extinction

- **makeup** (n) 짜임새, 구성
  composition; arrangement

- **intergovernmental** (adj) 정부간의
  occurring between two or more governments

- **panel** (n) 패널, 전문가 집단
  a group of people who plan or discuss an issue

- **spare** (v) 할애하다
  to give; grant

- **be in the same boat** (idiom) 같은 배를 탄 처지이다 (똑같은 곤경에 처해있다)
  to be in the same situation

- **frustration** (n) 불만, 좌절감
  disappointment; dissatisfaction

- **fire regulation** (n) 화재 규정
  rules or law related to preventing and controlling fire

- **petition** (n) 진정(서)
  a formal request to an authority; appeal

UNIT 2

- [ ] civilization
- [ ] enlightened
- [ ] merchant
- [ ] stretch across
- [ ] enslave
- [ ] indentured
- [ ] get rid of
- [ ] criminal
- [ ] sum up
- [ ] count on
- [ ] dominant
- [ ] brutality
- [ ] conquest
- [ ] profitable
- [ ] tunic
- [ ] baggy
- [ ] distinguish
- [ ] noblemen
- [ ] linen
- [ ] woolen
- [ ] woven
- [ ] monk
- [ ] nun
- [ ] freeze
- [ ] work out
- [ ] around the corner
- [ ] constitution
- [ ] motivation
- [ ] liberty
- [ ] democracy
- [ ] debt
- [ ] economic depression
- [ ] be reflected on
- [ ] representative
- [ ] creditor
- [ ] interfere
- [ ] gesture
- [ ] dull look
- [ ] appropriate
- [ ] interviewee
- [ ] non-verbal
- [ ] literally
- [ ] follow-up
- [ ] cross-examination
- [ ] drop by
- [ ] thesis
- [ ] archive
- [ ] restricted
- [ ] access
- [ ] relevant

- **civilization** (n) 문명
  an advanced state of cultural development in human society

- **enlightened** (adj) 개화된
  informed; open-minded; knowledgeable

- **merchant** (n) 상인
  tradesman; dealer; retailer

- **stretch across** 펼쳐지다
  to extend; spread

- **enslave** (v) 노예로 만들다
  to make into a slave

- **indentured** (adj) 계약 노동의
  forced to work for a period of time by some authority

- **get rid of** 없애다
  to waste; throw away; be free from

- **criminal** (n) 범죄자
  a person who is convicted of a crime; lawbreaker

- **sum up** 요약하다
  to add together

- **count on** 의지하다; 믿다, 확신하다
  to depend on; rely on

- **dominant** `adj` 우세한
  main; superior; primary

- **brutality** `n` 잔혹성
  cruel and violent treatment; cruelty; inhumanity

- **conquest** `n` 정복
  victory; takeover; invasion

- **profitable** `adj` 수익성이 있는
  money-making; beneficial; worthwhile

- **tunic** `n` 튜닉 (소매가 없는 헐렁한 웃옷)
  a sleeveless garment to be worn over other clothing

- **baggy** `adj` 헐렁한
  loose; oversize

- **distinguish** `v` 구별하다
  to differentiate; discriminate; tell apart

- **noblemen** `n` 상류층
  members of the nobility in earlier times

- **linen** `n` 리넨, 아마섬유
  a kind of cloth made from a plant called flax

- **woolen** `adj` 양모의, 모직의
  made from wool or a mixture of wool
  `n` 모직물, 모직 옷
  clothes made of wool

- **woven** adj 엮인, 짜인(weave의 과거분사형)
  (past participle of weave) knitted; braided

- **monk** n 수도자
  a member of a male religious community that is separated from the outside world

- **nun** adj 수녀
  a member of a female religious community

- **freeze** v 얼다, 얼리다; 냉동하다; 정지시키다
  to become hardened into ice; hold up; stop

- **work out** (일이) 풀리다, 잘 되다, 해결되다
  to solve; happen; turn out

- **around the corner** 아주 가까운
  nearby

- **constitution** n 헌법
  the system of laws which formally states people's rights and duties

- ☐ **motivation** (n) 동기
  incentive; reason; inspiration

- ☐ **liberty** (n) 자유
  freedom; independence

- ☐ **democracy** (n) 민주주의
  a system of government in which people choose their rulers by voting in elections

- ☐ **debt** (n) 빚
  a sum of money that you owe someone

- ☐ **economic depression**   경기 침체
  recession; economic decline

- ☐ **be reflected on**   반영되다
  to be shown; be indicated

- ☐ **representative** (n) 대표(자)
  agent; delegate

- ☐ **creditor** (n) 채권자
  a person who you owe money to

- ☐ **interfere** (v) 간섭하다
  to get involved although it is not wanted; intervene

- **gesture** (n) 몸짓
  signal; motion; sign

- **dull look** 지루한 표정
  a facial expression of boredom; plain or uninterested expression

- **appropriate** (adj) 적절한
  suitable; fitting; well-suited

- **interviewee** (n) 인터뷰 받는 사람, 면접 보는 사람
  a person who is answering the questions during an interview

- **non-verbal** (adj) 비언어적인, 말로 하지 않는
  without words; instead of speaking

- **literally** (adv) 말 그대로, 그야말로
  really; actually ↔ figuratively

- **follow-up** 후속 조치
  something that is done to continue or add to something done previously

- **cross-examination** 반대 신문(직접 신문이 끝난 후 상대방 당사자로부터 증인이 신문을 받는 것)
  questioning a witness already questioned by the opposing side especially during a trial

- **drop by** 잠깐 들르다
  to visit informally; come by

- **thesis** ⓝ 학위 논문; 논지
  a long written paper based on your own ideas and research; essay

- **archive** ⓝ (보관되어 있는) 기록
  a collection of documents and records containing historical information; chronicles

- **restricted** adj 제한된
  limited; confined

- **access** ⓝ 접근; 출입
  entry; permit to go into something or somewhere

- **relevant** adj 관련된; 적절한
  significant; appropriate; related

UNIT 3

- threat
- asteroid
- comet
- hazardous
- disastrous
- attempt
- blow
- detect
- systematic
- function
- refresh
- synapse
- downscale
- overload
- contrary
- notice
- maintenance
- be flattered
- invasive
- infrared light
- penetrate
- blood vessel
- metabolic
- consumption
- context
- exposed
- sustainable
- survey
- lost
- grasp
- vacuum dried
- appetizing
- simulate
- crop
- ingredient
- textured
- sprout
- manufacturing
- dismiss
- logging
- run through

- □ **threat** (n) 위협, 협박
  warning; hazard; risk

- □ **asteroid** (n) 소행성
  one of the numerous small planets that move around the sun between Mars and Jupiter

- □ **comet** (n) 혜성
  a bright object with a long tail that travels around the sun

- □ **hazardous** (adj) 위험한, 유해한
  dangerous; unsafe

- □ **disastrous** (adj) 비참한, 재난의
  terrible; devastating; tragic

- □ **attempt** (n) 시도
  effort
  (v) 시도하다, 꾀하다; ~에 도전하다
  to try; endeavour; undertake

- □ **blow** (v) 불어서 날리다; 폭파하다
  to expel; sweep; carry

- □ **detect** (v) 발견하다, 간파하다
  to notice; identify; recognize

- **systematic** adj 조직적인, 계통적인
  organized; orderly

- **function** n 기능
  assigned duty or activity; purpose

- **refresh** v 새롭게 하다, 상쾌하게 하다
  to revive; freshen; revitalize

- **synapse** n 시냅스(신경 세포의 연접부)
  one of the points in the nervous system at which a signal passes from one nerve cell to another

- **downscale** v 규모를 축소하다
  to reduce in scale

- **overload** v ~에 짐을 너무 많이 지우다, 지나치게 부하를 걸다
  to burden; weigh down; strain

- **contrary** adj 반대의, ~에 반대되는
  opposed; opposite; contradictory

- **notice** n 통지, 통보; 게시
  announcement; communication; notification

- **maintenance** n 관리, 유지, 점검
  care; keeping; preservation; repair

- **be flattered** 으쓱해지다, 우쭐해지다
  pleased about something that makes you feel important or special

- **invasive** adj 침입하는, 침습성의
  intrusive; interfering; unwanted

- **infrared light** 적외선
  a type of radiation that is similar to light but has a longer wavelength

- **penetrate** v 관통하다, 뚫고 들어가다
  to pierce; go through; enter

- **blood vessel** 혈관
  a narrow tube through which your blood flows

- **metabolic** adj (사람 또는 동물의) 신진 대사의
  related to the way the chemical processes in your body cause food to be used in an efficient way such as making new cells or providing energy

- **consumption** n 소비, 소모
  using up; exhausting something through use

- **context** n 전후 사정, 맥락
  circumstance; condition; situation

- **exposed** adj 노출된
  revealed; uncovered; unprotected

- **sustainable** adj 지속 가능한
  keeping in existence; maintaining

- **survey** n (설문) 조사
  examination; study; inquiry

- **lost** adj 길을 잃은; 어쩔 줄 모르는
  confused; disoriented; off-track

- **grasp** v 움켜쥐다; 파악하다
  to catch; understand; take in

- **vacuum dried** 진공 건조된
  having liquid material removed from a mixture under reduced air pressure

- **appetizing** adj 식욕을 돋우는
  tasty; delicious; tempting; appealing

- **simulate** v ~한 척 하다; 흉내내다
  to pretend; act; put on; make an imitation

- **crop** n (농)작물
  a plant that is grown in large quantities for food; produce; harvest

- **ingredient** (n) 재료, 성분, 구성 요소
  things that are used to make something especially when you are cooking

- **textured** (adj) 질감을 살린, 특별한 질감이 나게 만든
  having the surface made to have certain characteristics

- **sprout** (n) (식물의) 눈, 새싹
  a young plant growth such as a bud or a shoot

- **manufacturing** (adj) 제조(업)의
  being produced in a factory

- **dismiss** (v) 묵살하다, 무시하다
  to disregard; reject; ignore

- **logging** (n) 벌목
  the activity of cutting down trees

- **run through** 훑어 보다
  to go over; take a look; review

UNIT 4

- define
- anthropologist
- archeological
- cooperation
- intriguing
- spotted
- giggle
- groan
- stick to
- extensive
- pitch
- monotonous
- cub
- reassure
- sign in

- unload
- drag
- flash
- randomly
- recall
- wired into
- seeker
- neuroscientific
- extreme sports
- reward
- fill out
- imaging
- neural fiber
- residency
- check out

- burden
- spontaneous
- linguist
- pick up
- kindergarten
- acquisition
- linked
- rainforest
- weigh
- store
- get stuck
- custodian
- radiator
- rusty

- □ **define** v 정의하다, 규정하다
  to explain; characterize; describe

- □ **anthropologist** n 인류학자
  one who is involved in scientific studies of human culture

- □ **archeological** adj 고고학의
  of studies that involve people or societies of the past by examining the objects from that period

- □ **cooperation** n 협력, 협동
  collaboration; working together; support

- □ **intriguing** adj 흥미를 자아내는
  interesting; compelling; exciting

- □ **spotted** adj 얼룩덜룩한, 반점이 있는
  with spots (on skin or surface)

- □ **giggle** n 낄낄거리는 웃음
  a childlike laugh with repeated short sounds

- □ **groan** n 신음 소리, 끙끙거리는 소리
  a deep, inarticulate sound of pain or displeasure

- □ **stick to** ~을 계속하다; 고수하다
  to remain; keep; continue

- **extensive** adj 폭넓은; 대규모의
  wide; broad; large-scale; vast; widespread

- **pitch** n 음의 높낮이
  the distinctive quality of a sound

- **monotonous** adj 단조로운
  being regular; repeated without changes

- **cub** n (곰, 사자, 여우 등의) 새끼
  a young wild animal such as a lion, wolf or bear

- **reassure** v 안심시키다
  to put one's mind at rest; restore confidence to; encourage

- **sign in** 도착 시 서명하다; 서명하고 들어가다
  to officially record your arrival at a hotel or for an event

- **unload** v (짐을) 내리다
  to empty; unpack; discharge

- **drag** v 끌다, 끌고 가다
  to pull along with difficulty; bring by force

- **flash** v 잠깐 비치다, 휙 나타나다
  to show; display; appear suddenly

- **randomly** adv 무작위로
  without any specific pattern or purpose

- □ **recall** (v) 기억해 내다, 상기하다
  to remember; bring to mind

- □ **wired into** 입력된, 내재된
  determined or put into effect by physiological or neurological mechanisms

- □ **seeker** (n) ~을 추구하는 사람
  someone who is looking for or trying to get something

- □ **neuroscientific** (adj) 신경 과학의
  of or related to neuroscience

- □ **extreme sports** 익스트림 스포츠, 극한 스포츠
  types of sports involving high levels of risk

- □ **reward** (n) 보상
  repayment; return; prize

- □ **fill out** 기입하다
  to write information in the spaces of a form or document

- □ **imaging** (n) 이미지화
  the process of forming images; visualization of internal bodily organs

- □ **neural fiber** 신경 섬유
  a thin piece of flesh connecting nerve cells

- **residency** (n) 거주
  staying in a particular place

- **check out** 체크아웃, 퇴실하다
  to leave a hotel or clinic where you've been staying

- **burden** (v) 부담을 지우다
  to trouble; weigh down

- **spontaneous** (adj) 자발적인; 즉흥적인; 자연스러운
  unplanned; impulsive; natural; instinctive

- **linguist** (n) 언어학자
  someone who studies the science of language

- **pick up** 알게 되다, 익히다
  to learn; acquire

- **kindergarten** (n) 유치원
  an informal kind of school for very young children

- **acquisition** (n) 습득, 취득
  gaining possession of something

- **linked** adj 연결된, 연계된
  connected; associated

- **rainforest** n 우림
  a thick forest of tall trees found in tropical areas; jungle

- **weigh** v 무게가 나가다
  to have a weight of

- **store** v 저장하다, 비축하다
  to keep; reserve; deposit; save

- **get stuck** (갇히거나 빠져서) 꼼짝 못하다; 끼어 있다
  to not move

- **custodian** n 관리인
  a person who is officially in charge of something; caretaker; janitor

- **radiator** n 라디에이터, 방열기
  a hollow metal device connected to a central heating system

- **rusty** adj 녹슨, 녹투성이의
  oxidized; covered with a brown substance due to the contact with water or oxygen

:: UNIT 5

- [ ] genetic
- [ ] binocular
- [ ] domestication
- [ ] tame
- [ ] lactose
- [ ] alternative
- [ ] hydrogen
- [ ] worldwide
- [ ] take for granted
- [ ] sanitation service
- [ ] run for
- [ ] not one's cup of tea
- [ ] candidate
- [ ] fill in
- [ ] resume
- [ ] relatively
- [ ] ageing
- [ ] societal
- [ ] adaptation
- [ ] workforce
- [ ] stagnate
- [ ] boil down to
- [ ] leap
- [ ] estimate
- [ ] initiate
- [ ] reception
- [ ] keep in mind
- [ ] refundable
- [ ] show up
- [ ] souvenir
- [ ] abroad
- [ ] migration
- [ ] destination
- [ ] demographic
- [ ] pension
- [ ] harvest
- [ ] plow
- [ ] weed
- [ ] needless
- [ ] wage
- [ ] portion
- [ ] reluctant
- [ ] in debt
- [ ] injure
- [ ] in bad shape
- [ ] try one's luck
- [ ] fill in
- [ ] one's best shot

- **genetic** **adj** 유전의, 유전학의
  affecting or affected by genes

- **binocular** **adj** 두 눈으로 보는
  involving both eyes at the same time

- **domestication** **n** 사육; 재배
  bringing wild animals or plants under control and using them

- **tame** **v** 길들이다
  to control; discipline; train

- **lactose** **n** 락토오스, 유당
  a type of sugar found in milk and sometimes added to food

- **alternative** **adj** 양자 택일의; 대신의
  different; another; substitute

- **hydrogen** **n** 수소
  a colorless gas that is the lightest and most common element in the universe

- **worldwide** **adj** 세계적인
  globally; generally; universally

- **take for granted** 당연한 일로 생각하다; (익숙해져서) 가볍게 보다
  not to appreciate or value something

- **sanitation service** 위생 서비스
  a service for keeping facilities or dwelling clean and healthy

- **run for** 입후보하다
  to try to be elected

- **not one's cup of tea** **idiom** 취향이 아닌
  not something one enjoys

- **candidate** **n** 선거 출마자, 입후보자; 지원자
  contender; nominee; runner; competitor

- **fill in** ~에게 (정보를) 알려주다
  to supply (someone) with information; inform (someone) about something

- **resume** **v** 재개하다, 다시 시작하다
  to begin again; continue after an interruption

- **relatively** **adv** 비교적
  comparatively; somewhat; rather

- **ageing** **adj** 노화하는, 늙어가는
  boooming old

- **societal** **adj** 사회의
  relating to society or the way it is organized

Vocabulary •• 29

- **adaptation** (n) 적응; 각색
  conversion; adjustment; modification; naturalization

- **workforce** (n) 노동력, 노동 인구
  the total number of people in a country or region who are physically able to do a job and are available for work

- **stagnate** (v) 침체되다; 부진해지다
  to stop changing or progressing

- **boil down to** 핵심은 ~이다
  to reduce; summarize = come down to

- **leap** (n) 도약; 급증, 급등
  jump; sudden progress

- **estimate** (v) 추산하다, 추정하다
  to calculate roughly; evaluate; judge

- **initiate** (v) 개시되게 하다, 착수시키다
  to begin; open; set in motion

- **reception** (n) 접수처, 프론트
  a place where people are greeted for an event

- **keep in mind** (idiom) ~를 마음에 담아두다, 잊지 않고 있다
  to consider; remember

- **refundable** adj 환불 가능한
  being able to get the money back

- **show up** 나타나다, 눈에 띄다
  to come; attend; appear

- **souvenir** n 기념품
  something you buy or keep as a reminder of a holiday, place, or event

- **abroad** adv 해외에, 해외로
  overseas; out of the country

- **migration** n 이주, 이동
  moving from one place to another especially in order to find work or to live

- **destination** n 목적지, 도착지
  the place to which one is going or directed; journey's end; stop; station

- **demographic** adj 인구 통계학적인
  relating to or concerning the study of the characteristics of human population

- **pension** (n) 연금; 생활 보조금, 수당
  allowance; benefit

- **harvest** (n) 수확; 수확물
  the gathering of a crop; produce; yield

- **plow** (v) 쟁기로 갈다
  to turn over the soil using a farming tool called a plow

- **weed** (v) 잡초를 뽑다
  to remove weeds from field or garden

- **needless** (adj) 불필요한
  unnecessary; without any use; pointless

- **wage** (n) 임금, 급료
  amount of money paid regularly for someone's work

- **portion** (n) 부분; 몫
  section; share; part

- **reluctant** (adj) 꺼리는, 마지못한, 주저하는
  unwilling; hesitant; unenthusiastic

- **in debt** 빚을 진
  owing someone money or a favor

- **injure** (v) 부상을 입다
  to hurt; damage; wound

- ☐ **in bad shape** 쇠약한, 상태가 좋지 않은
  not in good (physical or situational) condition

- ☐ **try one's luck** `idiom` 운을 시험해 보다
  to see if things will work out as one desires

- ☐ **fill in** (~의 자리를 잠깐) 대신하다
  to substitute; replace; take the place of

- ☐ **one's best shot** 최대로 노력하기, 최선을 다하기
  one's best effort; the best one can do

UNIT 6

- expert
- classify
- genre
- rooted
- slum
- peak
- die down
- popularity
- on end
- equivalent
- title
- radical
- prominent
- theorist
- incorporate
- athleticism
- free-flowing
- vitality
- overdue
- drop off
- accounting
- owe
- mixed up
- thatched
- skeleton
- reed
- straw
- roofing
- flexible
- bend
- lifespan
- insulative
- misconception
- landscape
- majority
- harsh
- patron
- spawn
- multitude
- alter
- available
- extend
- panic
- lighting
- conserve
- earth
- ventilation
- cutting-edge
- barley
- porridge
- spice
- feast
- seated
- meal plan
- rate
- commuter

- **expert** n 전문가
  a person with a high degree of skill in or knowledge of a subject

- **classify** v 분류하다, 구분하다
  to organize according to category

- **genre** n 장르
  a particular type of literature, painting, music, or other art form

- **rooted** adj ~에 뿌리를 둔
  based; embedded; ingrained

- **slum** n 빈민가, 슬럼
  an area of a city where living conditions are very bad; ghetto; hovel

- **peak** n 절정, 정점
  high point; climax; summit; top

- **die down** 잦아들다, 약해지다
  to become less intense

- **popularity** (n) 인기
  the quality or state of being popular

- **on end** (어떤 기간 동안) 계속
  continuously; without stopping

- **equivalent** (n) 등가물, (~에) 상당하는 것
  something that is essentially equal to another or has similar effects; equal; match

- **title** (n) 제목, 표제
  a descriptive name

- **radical** (adj) 급진적인, 과격한; 철저한
  extreme; drastic; complete

- **prominent** (adj) 중요한; 유명한; 눈에 잘 띄는
  widely known; famous; distinguished

- **theorist** (n) 이론가
  someone who develops an abstract idea or set of ideas about a particular subject

- **incorporate** (v) 포함하다
  to include; assimilate; integrate

- **athleticism** (n) 스포츠열; 정열적인 활동성
  someone's fitness and ability to perform well at sports or other physical activities

- **free-flowing** 자유롭게 흐르는
  moving with smooth and unbroken motion

- **vitality** (n) 활력
  energy; liveliness; strength

- **overdue** (adj) 기한이 지난
  past the deadline

- **drop off** (보통 어딘가로 가는 길에 사람이나 물건을) 내려 주다, 갖다 주다
  to quickly deposit or deliver ↔ pick up

- **accounting** (n) 회계
  the activity of keeping detailed records of money received and spent

- **owe** (v) 빚지고 있다; 신세를 지고 있다
  to be in debt; be obligated

- **mixed up** 혼란스러운
  confused

- ☐ **thatched** **adj** 짚으로 이은
  covered with straw or reeds

- ☐ **skeleton** **n** 뼈대, 골격
  framework; outline; structure

- ☐ **reed** **n** 갈대
  a tall plant with a strong hollow stem that can be used for making things such as baskets

- ☐ **straw** **n** 짚, 지푸라기
  dried yellowish stalks from crops

- ☐ **roofing** **n** 지붕 공사
  the work of putting new roofs on houses

- ☐ **flexible** **adj** 신축성 있는
  being able to bend easily without breaking

- ☐ **bend** **v** 굽히다, 숙이다, 구부리다
  to curve; lean; turn

- ☐ **lifespan** **n** 수명
  the period of time in which living organisms are normally expected to live

- **insulative** adj 절연, 단열, 방음 처리의
  serving to insulate; keeping safe

- **misconception** n 오해
  an idea that is not correct; error; misunderstanding

- **landscape** n 풍경
  outdoor scenes; scenery

- **majority** n 다수
  greater part; common

- **harsh** adj 가혹한, 냉혹한
  cruel; unkind; severe; rough

- **patron** n 후원자; 고객
  supporter; benefactor; sponsor

- **spawn** v (알 등을) 낳다; (어떤 결과나 상황을) 낳다
  to produce; generate

- **multitude** n 아주 많은 수, 다수
  mass; a great many; a large number

- **alter** v 변하다, 달라지다; 바꾸다, 고치다
  to change; modify

- **available** adj 구할 수 있는, 이용할 수 있는
  accessible; at hand; ready

- **extend** ⓥ 연장하다, 확대하다
  to lengthen; make longer; add to

- **panic** ⓥ 겁에 질려 어쩔 줄 모르다, 공황 상태에 빠지다
  to become hysterical; lose one's nerve; fear

- **lighting** ⓝ 조명
  the way a place is lit or the quality of the light in it

- **conserve** ⓥ 아끼다, 아껴 쓰다; 보호하다
  to save; reserve

- **earth** ⓝ 지면; 흙
  soil; clay; dirt

- **ventilation** ⓝ 통풍, 환기
  allowing fresh air to get into a room or building

- **cutting-edge** 최첨단의
  foremost; forefront; highly advanced

- **barley** ⓝ 보리
  a grain that is used to make food, beer, and whisky

- **porridge** ⓝ 포리지(귀리에 우유나 물을 부어 걸쭉하게 죽처럼 끓인 음식)
  a hot, thick and sticky food made with grain and water or milk

- **spice** (n) 양념, 향신료
  a variety of powder made from plants to put in food to add flavor

- **feast** (n) 연회, 잔치
  banquet; dinner; buffet

- **seated** (adj) 앉은, 자리 잡은
  placed; settled

- **meal plan** 정기 식사권
  an arrangement to have one's meal served on a regular basis

- **rate** (n) 요금, ~료
  price; cost; charge

- **commuter** (n) 통근자
  someone who travels a long distance every day to get to work or school

:: Actual Test

- [ ] fence
- [ ] strand
- [ ] mass produce
- [ ] cattle ranch
- [ ] intruder
- [ ] graze
- [ ] herd
- [ ] roam
- [ ] rail
- [ ] literary
- [ ] irony
- [ ] deny
- [ ] intellectual
- [ ] neutral
- [ ] horror
- [ ] relieved
- [ ] nationalism
- [ ] materialism
- [ ] rationalism
- [ ] forum
- [ ] contribute to
- [ ] proclaim
- [ ] disgusted
- [ ] enthusiasm
- [ ] dissolve
- [ ] visible
- [ ] nicotine
- [ ] reference
- [ ] deserve
- [ ] consistent
- [ ] emission
- [ ] methane
- [ ] potent
- [ ] manure
- [ ] decompose
- [ ] go easy on
- [ ] nutrient
- [ ] trigger
- [ ] snap shut
- [ ] ingest
- [ ] mechanical
- [ ] imitate
- [ ] humidity
- [ ] spoil
- [ ] objective
- [ ] committed
- [ ] priority
- [ ] give someone a push
- [ ] text

- □ **fence** ⓝ 울타리
  barrier; hedge; wall

- □ **strand** ⓝ 가닥
  string; fiber; thread

- □ **mass produce** 대량 생산하다
  to make a product in large quantity or scale

- □ **cattle ranch** (가축의) 방목장
  a large farm used for raising animals such as horses, cows or sheep

- □ **intruder** ⓝ 불법 침입자, 불청객
  a person who goes into a place where they are not supposed to be

- □ **graze** ⓥ (소, 양 등을) 방목하다
  to feed (animals and such) on growing grass

- □ **herd** ⓝ (동종 짐승의) 떼; (같은 류의 한 무리의) 사람들
  a large group of animals of one kind that live together

- □ **roam** ⓥ 돌아다니다, 배회하다
  to wander; stray; travel

- **rail** (n) 난간
  a horizontal bar attached to posts which acts as a fence or support

- **literary** (adj) 문학의; 문학적인
  concerned or connected with the writing, study, or appreciation of literature

- **irony** (n) 아이러니, 역설
  an odd or amusing situation that involves a contrast
  =paradox

- **deny** (v) 부정하다, 부인하다
  to refuse; reject; disclaim; disagree with

- **intellectual** (n) 지식인, 식자
  thinker; academic

- **neutral** (adj) 중립적인
  unbiased; impartial; uninvolved

- **horror** (n) 공포, 경악
  terror; fear; panic

- **relieved** adj 안도하는, 다행으로 여기는
  being free from something unpleasant

- **nationalism** n 민족주의; 애국심, 국수주의
  the strong belief that the interests of a particular nation-state are of primary importance

- **materialism** n 물질(만능)주의; 유물론
  the attitude of someone who greatly values money and wants to possess a lot of material things

- **rationalism** n 이성주의, 합리주의
  the belief that one's life should be based on reason and logic rather than emotion and religious beliefs

- **forum** n 포럼, 토론회
  a place, situation or group in which people exchange ideas and discuss issues

- **contribute to** 기부하다, 기여하다
  to be partly responsible for; help to cause something; lead to

- **proclaim** (v) 선언하다, 선포하다
  to declare; announce; make known

- **disgusted** (adj) 혐오감을 느끼는, 역겨워 하는
  feeling a strong sense of dislike or disapproval; offended; sickened; repulsed

- **enthusiasm** (n) 열광, 열정
  eagerness; interest; passion; zeal

- **dissolve** (v) 녹다, 용해되다; 끝내다; 사라지다, 흩어지다
  to end; break up; discontinue; terminate

- **visible** (adj) 보이는, 알아 볼 수 있는
  in view; apparent; can be seen

- **nicotine** (n) 니코틴
  the substance in tobacco that people can become addicted to

- **reference** (n) 참고 문헌
  a book or material to look at to find specific information or facts about a subject

- **deserve** (v) ~를 받을 만하다; 누릴 만하다
  to be worthy of; earn; justify

- **consistent** `adj` 한결 같은, 일관된
  unchanging; dependable; steady

- **emission** `n` 배출
  a substance discharge into the air; giving off; discharge

- **methane** `n` 메탄
  a colorless gas that has no smell

- **potent** `adj` 강한
  strong; powerful; vigorous

- **manure** `n` (동물의) 분뇨; (동물의 배설물로 만든) 거름
  animal droppings that is spread on the ground in order to make plants grow healthy and strong; compost

- **decompose** `v` 분해되다, 부패하다
  to decay; rot; break up

- **go easy on** `idiom` ~를 너무 많이 쓰지 않다
  to use something sparingly; try not to take too much

- **nutrient** `n` 영양소, 영양분
  a substance that help plants and animals grow

- **trigger** `v` 촉발시키다; 작동시키다
  to activate; provoke; set off; start

- **snap shut** 탁 닫다
  to close suddenly

- **ingest** v 삼키다, 먹다
  to take or absorb substance into the body

- **mechanical** adj 기계로 작동되는; 기계적인
  machinelike

- **imitate** v 모방하다, 본뜨다; 흉내내다
  to copy; simulate; follow

- **humidity** n 습도; 습기
  dampness; moisture; wetness

- **spoil** v 망치다, 버려 놓다
  to ruin; damage; rot; destroy

- **objective** n 목적, 목표
  purpose; aim; goal

- **committed** adj 헌신적인, 열성적인
  performing responsibly or having such attitude

- **priority** n 우선 사항; 우선권
  rank; an order of importance or urgency

- **give someone a push** idiom 밀어주다, 도와주다
  to pressure or motivate someone to act

- **text** v (휴대전화로) 문자를 보내다
  to exchange brief written messages between mobile phones

Script & Answer Keys

Unit 1 | Academic Lectures: Natural Science | Conversations

Practices

Warm Up

Answer Key

1. ants, colonies
2. earthquakes
3. dinosaurs, meteorite
4. emotions
5. features, survival
6. endangered, polar bears

Part I

Practice 1

Listening Script

Prof(W): Scientists have noticed that ants tend to <u>specialize</u> in jobs within their <u>colonies</u>. However, they also noticed that having the specialty doesn't necessarily make them <u>better workers</u>. A group of biologists studied rock ants to <u>figure out</u> how they actually work. In one of their experiments, they forced the <u>entire</u> colony of rock ants to <u>move</u> to a new artificial nest. When they moved, there were certain ants that specialized in carrying the larvae as their <u>only</u> job, but there were also others that did various jobs <u>in addition to</u> carrying larvae. So, the biologists <u>compared</u> the two groups of ants for the <u>amount</u> and the <u>speed</u> of their work. They found that the ants that only carried larvae were not working faster or better than other ants. So, they concluded that specialized ants weren't any more <u>efficient</u> than ants that do every job in the colony.

Q. What does the speaker mainly discuss?

Answer Key Ⓒ

Practice 2

Listening Script

Prof(M): In the early 20th century, scientists discovered seismic waves which are the vibrations <u>caused by</u> earthquakes. They found that seismic waves traveled thousands of miles through the <u>inside</u> of the Earth. This discovery was <u>important</u> to geologists because it helped them study and gain a more <u>accurate</u> picture of the Earth's interior. Geologists concluded that these vibrations were of two types: <u>compression</u>, or P waves and <u>shear</u>, or S waves. So, P waves travel through both <u>liquids</u> and solids while S waves travel only through solid materials. They also found that P waves <u>slowed down</u> at a certain depth but still continued traveling <u>deeper</u> into the Earth's interior. On the other hand, S waves disappeared or were <u>reflected</u> back. Eventually, geologists were able to <u>estimate</u> the depth of the <u>boundary</u> between the solid mantle and the liquid core within the Earth's interior.

Q. What is the main topic of the lecture?

Answer Key Ⓐ

📖 Practice 3
Listening Script

W: Excuse me. I need to <u>make</u> a course change. Can you help me with that?

M: Yes, but you should know that the <u>deadline</u> to add courses has already <u>passed</u>.

W: Oh, I see. But, I just need to <u>drop</u> a course. I can still do that, can't I?

M: Sure, you can. May I ask why, <u>though</u>?

W: Well, I thought I could <u>handle</u> six courses in a semester. But, it is a little <u>overwhelming</u>.

M: Six is a lot indeed. Well, dropping a course might be a <u>wise</u> decision then.

W: Yeah. So, I'm dropping one of my <u>electives</u>.

W: Okay. Now, let me just <u>log onto</u> the system here. And, I'll need your student ID number.

Q. What is the student's problem?
Answer Key ⓒ

Part II

📖 Practice 4
Listening Script

Prof(W): Many scientists have been trying hard to find an answer to why the dinosaurs disappeared from the Earth. Until very recently, many scientists believed that the dinosaurs were killed by a massive impact of a meteorite in the Yucatan. In case you don't know, the Yucatan is a peninsula located in Mexico. It is believed that this impact by a space rock was in fact the direct cause of a mass extinction of species, including the dinosaurs. But Geologist Gerta Keller disagrees with this belief and raises a new theory on the question. Based on her 20 years of research, she believes that the impact happened 300 thousand years after the dinosaurs disappeared. Therefore, she claims that it was not the impact of a meteorite but the volcanoes that probably killed the dinosaurs. According to Keller, there was a series of volcanic eruptions called Deccan Volcanism. It happened on India's Deccan plateau between 63 and 67 million years ago. The volcanoes emitted great amounts of sulfur dioxide into the atmosphere. Keller and her research team studied geologic samples from the area. They found less and less evidence of life after each subsequent volcanic eruption. This means, as Keller argues, the series of Deccan eruptions caused the mass extinction of life on the planet, including the dinosaurs.

Q1. What is the main topic of the lecture?
Q2. What does the speaker say about the massive impact by a space rock?
Q3. What did the research team find in studying Deccan Volcanism?

Answer Key

A Q1. Ⓑ   Q2. Ⓓ   Q3. Ⓑ

B 1. **Why**   2. **meteorite**   3. **peninsula**

4. **extinction** 5. **after** 6. **atmosphere**
7. **evidence**

📖 Practice 5
Listening Script

Prof(M): Many people ask questions about whether animals really feel sadness, joy, grief or embarrassment, you know, just like humans. Some people argue that animals do not really have emotions but we humans try to assign our own emotions to them. Well, I believe that animals do have emotions though it may not be as specific or sophisticated as human emotions. Actually, a biologist from the University of Colorado conducted an interesting research on this question. He spent over four thousand hours observing the behavior of wild as well as captive animals. Then, he mixed his observational data with neuroscience to make some scientific sense of it. He suggests that animal emotions are probably not different from human emotions. He believes that they express or release their emotions in a way that is richer and deeper than humans. That's perhaps because animals get completely absorbed in the moment and don't know what might happen by showing their joy or grief. Oh, by the way, he also makes an interesting suggestion based on his research. He believes that animals, at least some of the time, know right from wrong and behave accordingly. If you're interested in more specific results of his research, I suggest you go to his website and check it out. Uh, I'll write the address on the board.

Q1. What does the speaker mainly discuss?
Q2. What does the speaker say about animal emotions?
Q3. What does the speaker suggest to the students?

Answer Key

A Q1. Ⓑ Q2. Ⓓ Q3. Ⓒ
B 1. **specific** 2. **research** 3. **captive**
4. **different** 5. **deeper** 6. **absorbed**
7. **wrong** 8. **website**

📖 Practice 6
Listening Script

M: Hi, I'm here to change my major. Who do I need to talk to?

W: That would be me. Now, what's your current major?

M: It's mathematics. And, I'd like to change it to archaeology.

W: Wow, that's a big change. Were you unhappy with mathematics?

M: Well, I was doing okay with it. But, last semester, I took a couple of archaeology courses as electives. You know, just for fun.

W: And I guess you really liked it?

M: Yeah, totally. So, I decided that I'd rather study something I feel more passionate about.

W: I see. Well, in order to change your major, you have to submit a formal request.

M: I understand, and how should I do that? Is there a specific form?

W: Yes, wait a minute..., okay, here is the request form and you'll need the signatures of the chairperson from both the mathematics and archaeology departments.

M: Um, do I hand in this form here after I do that?

W: Of course. Bring it back to the registrar's office.

Q1. Why did the student come to the office?
Q2. Why does the student want to study archaeology?

Answer Key

A Q1. Ⓓ Q2. Ⓑ

B 1. **major** 2. **mathematics** 3. **archaeology**
4. **passionate** 5. **formal** 6. **chairperson**
7. **registrar's**

Test 1

Listening Script

Listen to part of a lecture in a science class.

Prof(W): The extinction of the dinosaurs has long been a fascinating subject for many scientists. The fact that they were such a large species and disappeared from earth rather suddenly makes it even more interesting to study. However, what I'd like to focus on today is not the extinction but the rise of the dinosaurs. Many people think that the dinosaurs rose to become so prevalent because they were superior to other animals. But, many scientists are saying that the dinosaurs were just lucky, and not superior enough to open the age of dinosaurs. According to the research, there was a mass extinction event about 200 million years ago at the end of Triassic period. At the time, the dinosaurs were in competition with ancient crocodiles called crurotarsans. In fact, the crurotarsans were supposed to be more diverse and more adaptable, in other words, more advanced as a species than the dinosaurs. However, for some reason, the crurotarsans didn't survive the extinction event in the late Triassic period while the dinosaurs did. The dinosaurs probably had a certain feature that helped in their survival even though they were not superior by nature. That's why scientists are now saying that the survival of the dinosaurs might have been just a lucky coincidence. From this, we can say that evolution does not necessarily come in predictable order. In fact, luck can be a big part of it, too.

Now, get ready to answer the questions.

Q1. What is the main topic of the lecture?
Q2. According to the lecture, what is true about the crurotarsans? Click on 2 answers.
Q3. What do many scientists think about the dinosaurs?
Q4. According to the lecture, what happened about 200 million years ago?
Q5. What does the speaker say about evolution?

Answer Key

Q1. Ⓑ Q2. Ⓐ,Ⓒ Q3. Ⓒ Q4. Ⓒ Q5. Ⓓ

Test 2

Listening Script

Listen to part of a lecture in a climatology class.

Prof(M): Many scientists are worried that the change in the climate will bring shifts in animal habitats. In other words, the increase in global temperature is causing animals to change where they live. Actually, we haven't really had that much increase in temperature yet. We've only had approximately 1 degree Fahrenheit or so within the last few decades. However, we're already beginning to see its impacts in most animal systems around the world. One case in point is how butterflies in every continent are on the move. According to one biologist, about 40% of butterfly species are changing their habitats. Likewise, many animals are moving up mountains and up towards the poles where the temperature is a little cooler. Also, about 60 % of species have changed the timing of when they do things in spring. For example, the timing for caterpillars to emerge is changing because leaves emerge at different times now due to climate change.

Climate change is also making it more difficult to preserve endangered species such as polar bears. Now, I mentioned earlier that animals are moving up to cooler regions. So, polar species including polar bears don't have anywhere to go. And they're very likely to die off unless a radical approach is made soon in order to protect them.

Scientists say that another 2 degrees warming might bring more critical changes in where and when animals move. And if it gets up to 6 degrees warmer, that means Earth's atmosphere has changed significantly. Then, we might go back to a time when there was a completely different makeup of plants and animals on our planet. An organization called IPCC, which stands for intergovernmental panel for climate change, has predicted the planet will continue to warm up from 4 to 11 degrees Fahrenheit in this century. Pretty frightening prediction, isn't it?

Now, get ready to answer the questions.

Q1. What does the speaker mainly discuss?
Q2. What is the main point of the talk?
Q3. According to the talk, how much has global temperature increased?
Q4. Why does the speaker mention butterflies?
Q5. What is happening to many animal species? Click on 2 answers.

Answer Key

Q1. Ⓑ Q2. Ⓒ Q3. Ⓐ Q4. Ⓓ Q5. Ⓒ, Ⓓ

Test 3

Listening Script

Listen to part of a conversation between a student and a professor.

W: Professor Mayfield, do you have a few minutes you can spare?

M: Yes, I think so. Come on in.

W: I'm sorry to drop by like this, but I didn't know when your office hours were.

M: That's fine. What can I do for you?

W: Um, my name is Anna and I'm trying to register for your history 201 class.

M: You mean the war history course?

W: Yes. But, I couldn't get in because it's already full.

M: Oh, that's news to me. That course has never been full before.

W: *Then, you will be surprised to know that there are many who are in the same boat as me.*

M: Huh, really? Well, the assigned classroom was quite small because we didn't think it would be so popular.

W: But, I really need this course to complete my requirement as a history major.

M: I understand your frustration. But, I can't just let people in especially because of the fire regulation for classrooms.

W: Can't the history department find a bigger classroom for it? I can even get people to sign a petition.

M: Hmm, I suppose. Tell you what, I'll make the same request to the department secretary as well. I mean, it wouldn't hurt to try.

W: That would be great. Thanks.

M: Well, I hope to see you in the class.

Now, get ready to answer the questions.

Q1. What is the student's problem?

Q2. What does the professor say about history 201?

Q3. What does the student mean when she says this:
"Then, you will be surprised to know that there are many who are in the same boat as me."

Q4. What does the professor say he will do?

Answer Key

Q1. Ⓑ   Q2. Ⓑ   Q3. Ⓑ   Q4. Ⓒ

Listening Helper

Answer Key

A 1. **efficient**   2. **seismic**   3. **assign**
   4. **conducted** 5. **passionate** 6. **coincidences**
   7. **emerge**   8. **spare**   9. **frustrations**
   10. **petition**

B 1. **figure out,** Ⓑ   2. **artificial,** Ⓐ
   3. **get, absorbed,** Ⓒ   4. **submit,** Ⓑ
   5. **superior,** Ⓐ   6. **impact,** Ⓒ
   7. **subsequent,** Ⓐ   8. **prevalent,** Ⓐ
   9. **elective,** Ⓑ   10. **overwhelming,** Ⓐ

| Unit 2 | Academic Lectures: History Conversations |

Practices

Warm Up

Answer Key

1. **passage, deserts**
2. **black Americans, slaves**
3. **small, military**
4. **status, past**

5. representatives, Constitution

6. interview, historical

Part I

🔊 Practice 1
Listening Script

Prof(W): The Silk Road first began in China during the Han Dynasty around 130 B.C.E. The <u>emperor</u> named Wudi learned that there was a great civilization to the <u>west</u> of his empire. Until then, Chinese people didn't know about the <u>existence</u> of other civilizations besides their <u>own</u>. Now, being a wise and enlightened <u>ruler</u>, Wudi saw this new finding as the potential for trade between the two <u>cultures</u>. In order to make trade possible, Wudi began to develop a passage that led all the way to the <u>newly found</u> western civilization. This passage got its name 'silk road' because it was used by <u>merchants</u> who mainly brought silk from China to the West. Then <u>on their return</u> to China, they brought glasses, linen and gold from the West. The Silk Road <u>stretched across</u> about 5,000 miles of land and water including trails, bridges and deserts.

Q. Which of the following is true about the Silk Road? Click on 2 answers.
Answer Key Ⓐ, Ⓑ

🔊 Practice 2
Listening Script

Prof(M): <u>Contrary to</u> popular belief, the earliest generations of black Americans were not the <u>first</u> group of slaves in North America. When the Europeans first came to the new <u>territory</u> in the 16th century, they tried to <u>enslave</u> the native people. But, they were unsuccessful because most of the native people died of <u>sickness</u> when they were <u>enslaved</u>. Then the British government <u>forced</u> thousands of people to come to North America. These people were called indentured servants which was a kind of <u>temporary</u> slavery. It was actually a way for the government to <u>get rid of</u> the less desirable members of the society like <u>criminals</u>. Then the Europeans forced millions of African people to North America to work as slaves. In the early 1800s, there were <u>no more</u> Africans coming as slaves. However, the Africans who were already in North America <u>continued</u> their enslaved lives <u>until</u> the Civil War.

Q. The speaker mentioned the history of slavery in North America. Check if the following group of people was mentioned as slaves or not. Put a check mark in the correct box.
Answer Key
Mentioned: Ⓑ, Ⓒ, Ⓓ
Not mentioned: Ⓐ, Ⓔ

🔊 Practice 3
Listening Script

W: Hi, Professor. I think there is an <u>error</u> in my test score.

M: Oh? What could that be?

W: You gave me 80, but when I <u>sum</u>

up the marks from each question, I get a total of 82.

M: Hmm..., you are right. I guess my TA George made a mistake with the <u>math</u>.

W: Actually, I went to see George <u>first</u> at the TA's office. But he was not there.

M: Well, <u>leave</u> it with me and I'll <u>have him</u> fix your mark. I'm sorry that this happened.

W: No, no. <u>As long as</u> it gets fixed, that's no problem.

M: Well, you can <u>count on</u> me. I'll make sure of that.

Q. What problem does the student have?

Answer Key Ⓒ

Part II

🔊 Practice 4
Listening Script

Prof(M): In the early history of civilization, there were a number of important cultures that emerged around the same time period. Some of them were bigger and more powerful than others. So, naturally, the smaller civilizations were under the heavy influence of their... uh, I would say, more dominant neighbors. However, some of them became more important and influential through trade and military strategy. One good example would be the Aramaean civilization. Aramaeans were well known for their brutality and military conquests. And by around 1200 B.C.E., they were able to gain control over the trade routes between Egypt and Mesopotamia. You see, these trade routes were quite important for the Aramaeans. Why? Well, first of all, Egypt and Mesopotamia were the two most powerful and wealthy nations at that time. So, controlling the trade routes between them was greatly profitable. Also, people from other cultures who lived in the Aramaean controlled regions had no choice but to learn to speak their language, Aramaic. In fact, many portions of the Bible that were written in these regions were in Aramaic. So, the fact that their language was vastly used even outside their own culture probably helped the Aramaean civilization become more influential among other smaller civilizations.

Q1. What does the speaker mainly discuss?

Q2. According to the speaker, why was it important for Aramaeans to control the trade routes?
Click on 2 answers.

Q3. What does the speaker say about Egypt and Mesopotamia?

Answer Key

A Q1. Ⓑ Q2. Ⓐ, Ⓒ Q3. Ⓒ

B 1. **emerged** 2. **dominant** 3. **military**

4. **control** 5. **trade** 6. **learned**

7. **influential**

🔊 Practice 5
Listening Script

Prof(W): Most of what we know about Medieval European clothing comes from paintings and sculptures of the time. That's why I brought some slides of some of the medieval paintings to show you. Now, it seems that most people in Medieval Europe wore loose tunics like big baggy t-shirts made of linen or wool. But, clothing gradually became more complicated and used as a way to distinguish people with different status or professions. For example, most men usually wore tunics down to their knees. Old men and monks, however, wore their tunics down to the ground. Kings and noblemen also wore long tunics for special occasions like parties and ceremonies. A lot of men especially those who rode horses and lived in cooler climate wore wool pants under their tunics. But, noblemen did not wear pants, rather, they wore woven tights under their tunics. Now, how about women? Well, women also wore different kinds of clothes depending on their status. Most women wore two layers of tunic, a linen under tunic and a woolen over tunic. Women sometimes wore woven tights or socks on their legs, but they never wore pants. Noblewomen often wore fancy tall hats with colorful tunics as you can see in this picture. However, the tunics nuns wore were generally in black or white.

Q1. What is the main topic of the lecture?
Q2. Why did the speaker bring the slides of medieval paintings?
Q3. According to the lecture, how did noblewomen dress?

Answer Key

A Q1. Ⓒ Q2. Ⓒ Q3. Ⓒ

B 1. **paintings** 2. **loose** 3. **distinguish**
4. **knees** 5. **long** 6. **woven** 7. **legs**
8. **colorful**

Practice 6
Listening Script

W: You look worried. What's the matter?

M: I'm worried about my German. I almost failed my speech test.

W: Oh no, I thought you were really enjoying your German class.

M: I still enjoy it, especially the grammar. But, I just freeze when I'm supposed to speak the language.

W: Hmm, maybe you need to practice with a native German speaker.

M: I think I should. But, I don't know anyone around me who can speak German.

W: Well, I do. One of My cousins just moved from Germany. I'm sure he can be your tutor.

M: Oh....

W: Actually, you know what? He's looking for a math tutor, and....

M: Really? You know I've been tutoring math for two years.

W: Well, that's exactly my point. So, it may work out perfectly for both of you.

M: I sure hope so. How can I meet him?

W: Well, why don't I just call him now? He lives just around the corner. Maybe we can see him right away.

M: Wow, really? That'll be great.

Q1. What is the conversation mainly about?
Q2. What does the man hope to do with the woman's cousin?
Q3. How can the man help her cousin?

Answer Key

A Q1. Ⓐ Q2. Ⓐ Q3. Ⓑ

B 1. **Failed** 2. **grammar** 3. **Practice** 4. **math**
 5. **Tutored** 6. **corner**

Test 1

Listening Script

Listen to part of a lecture given in a history class.

Prof(W): As you know, the United States Constitution was written back in 1787 by the representatives from each state. Now, historians have two different points of view about the motivation behind writing the Constitution. The first one I'm going to tell you is called the idealist view. The idealists say that the Constitution writers were motivated by ideas of the revolutionary war. The ideas, of course, were liberty and democracy. They also believe that the writers were concerned about the problems the United States had at that time. What kind of problems? Well, it was a young country with an economic depression, a large amount of debt caused by the war and major social chaos. So, according to the historians supporting the idealist view, the writers' need to control these problems was also reflected in the Constitution. The other point of view is the economic view. The historians with the economic view argue that the writers were motivated by their own financial interests. As a matter of fact, most writers were quite wealthy. The historians argue that these wealthy representatives didn't want to lose their money under the new governing system. So, they wanted a strong government that protects private property and encourage business for their own benefit. The economic view also points out that the government borrowed money from some of the Constitution writers during the war. As creditors, the writers wanted the government to pay off the large war debts by collecting taxes. Therefore, according to the economic view, the writers wanted a Constitution that allowed such a strong central government. Now, it's difficult to decide which view is right. I'd say neither view is completely accurate. In fact, I believe that both the idealist and the economic view perhaps can be parts of the whole picture.

Now, get ready to answer the questions.

Q1. What does the speaker mainly discuss?
Q2. Who were the writers of the United States Constitution?
Q3. According to the historians with the economic view, why did the Constitution writers encourage the government to pay off the war debt?
Q4. The speaker mentions the following statements as to what the Constitution writers wanted. Indicate whether they are part of the idealist or the economic view. Put a check

mark in the correct box.

Q5. What does the speaker say about the different views on the motivations behind the writing of the Constitution?

Answer Key

Q1. Ⓒ Q2. Ⓑ Q3. Ⓐ

Q4. **Idealist view:** Ⓐ, Ⓓ
     Economic view: Ⓑ, Ⓒ

Q5. Ⓑ

Test 2

Listening Script

Listen to part of a lecture given by a history teacher.

Prof(M): As a student of history, you sometimes need to interview people to learn about their personal experiences during historical events. When you do, there are five important things you need to remember and I'd like to go through them with you. First, you have to give them voice. You know, let them tell their stories. You're not trying to get them to tell the truth or give an accurate description of the event. It's better to ask questions that are open-ended so that they can tell their stories. For example..., um, let's say you're interviewing someone who experienced the Great Depression in the 1930s. Instead of asking 'Was the Great Depression a difficult time?' you may ask, 'What do you remember the most about the Great Depression?' *Get it?* Secondly, you should remember to give them the space to operate. This means that you don't interfere every two minutes to say things like 'Oh, really? Tell me more.'

Instead, you may give them facial expressions, body gestures to encourage them to continue with their story. The third one for you to remember is to make sure you're enjoying it. This is actually quite important. If you sit there with a dull look on your face, the interviewee will be discouraged thinking that you're bored with the story. So, interact with the interviewee in non-verbal ways. Appropriate facial expressions or body gestures will be helpful. The fourth one is to write down the follow-up questions. When they get excited, people sometimes go on and on with their stories, sometimes for over an hour! Literally, you can't stop them. So, instead of breaking the story, just write down the questions and ask them after awhile. Now, the last one is to be understanding. I mean, you're asking them to open up and share their personal stories. So, they may feel uncomfortable with it. If they don't want to discuss it, you should never force them to. You're doing an interview, not a cross-examination. So, try to be sensitive.

Now, get ready to answer the questions.

Q1. What is the main topic of the lecture?

Q2. What does the speaker say about asking questions during an interview?

Q3. What does the speaker mean when he says this:
"Get it?"

Q4. The speaker mentions the following things about interviewing people. Indicate whether each of them is appropriate to do or not to do during an interview. Put a check mark in the correct box.

Q5. Why does the speaker say it is

important to be sensitive during an interview?

Answer Key

Q1. Ⓐ Q2. Ⓒ Q3. Ⓑ
Q4. **To do:** Ⓐ, Ⓑ, Ⓔ **Not to do:** Ⓒ, Ⓓ
Q5. Ⓓ

Test 3

Listening Script

Listen to a conversation between a student and a professor.

W: Professor Wilson, can I come in?

M: Oh, hi, Amanda. I was waiting for you. Come on in.

W: Thank you for meeting with me. I know you're very busy these days.

M: Well, I am. But, I'm glad that you dropped by. So, how's your thesis going?

W: It's going all right. Um, actually, that's why I asked to meet with you.

M: Any problem?

W: Well, there's a really old article I'd like to read from our university online archives. But it's under the restricted section so I can't access the file.

M: I see. I supposed you'd like me to print it out for you, right?

W: Well, yeah... if it's not too much trouble for you.

M: No trouble at all. Don't worry. By the way, what is the article about?

W: Um, I only read its summary. It seems that the article analyzes the changes in career choices for university graduates during World War II.

M: Oh, that sounds interesting.

W: It does. And more importantly, it's quite relevant to my thesis topic.

M: Well, good for you. All right, why don't I just get it printed while you are here?

W: Great. Thank you so much for your help, Professor. Wilson.

M: *Uh, don't mention it.*

Now, get ready to answer the questions.

Q1. Why does the woman come to see the man?

Q2. What is the woman's problem?

Q3. What is the man going to do for the woman?

Q4. What is the man's attitude when he says this:
"Uh, don't mention it."

Answer Key

Q1. Ⓐ Q2. Ⓓ Q3. Ⓑ Q4. Ⓒ

Listening Helper

Answer Key

A 1. **dominant**   2. **conquests**   3. **baggy**
  4. **gestures**   5. **creditors**   6. **freeze-up**
  7. **count on**   8. **enslave**   9. **get rid of**
  10. **archives**

B 1. **stretched,** Ⓒ 2. **motivation,** Ⓐ
  3. **interfere,** Ⓑ 4. **enlightened,** Ⓒ
  5. **distinguish,** Ⓐ 6. **sum up,** Ⓐ
  7. **literally,** Ⓑ 8. **reflected in,** Ⓐ
  9. **around the corner,** Ⓒ 10. **drop by,** Ⓐ

Unit 3 | Academic Lectures: Applied Sciences
Conversations

Practices

Warm Up

Answer Key

1. Astronomers, crash
2. sleep, brain
3. missions, oxygen
4. cell phones, everywhere
5. vacuum
6. recycle

Part I

🔊 Practice 1

Listening Script

Prof(W): Nowadays, we hear more and more about the threat of asteroid and comet strikes on Earth. Astronomers and space scientists are trying to track potentially hazardous asteroids that could cause a disastrous impact on our planet. We've seen some science fiction movies or fiction illustrating people's attempts to blow the asteroid into small pieces. However, according to the experts in real life, such attempts would be far too expensive and dangerous. They say that if a killer asteroid were detected, changing its course would be the most critical step to take to prevent it from hitting the Earth. In any case, it is extremely important to monitor the existing objects in space continuously and accurately. However, many experts say that there are not enough funds provided to conduct even a systematic scan of the sky.

Q. Why does the speaker mention people's attempts to blow up an asteroid?

Answer Key Ⓑ

🔊 Practice 2

Listening Script

Prof(M): There's no doubt that we need a good amount of sleep to be able to function properly. But, why? Why do we feel refreshed when we wake up from our sleep? Sleep experts mostly agree that sleep is important for the functioning of our brain, especially our memory. However, they disagree why and how it helps our memory. One group of experts believes that we need sleep to refresh our synapses, which connect brain cells. According to them, we need to downscale synapses through our sleep. Otherwise, synapses become too strong and get overloaded in their ability to learn and remember. So, by going to sleep, your brain will be refreshed and ready to learn again. However, the other group of experts thinks quite the contrary. They believe we need sleep to replay and strengthen synapses which have been used while we were learning during waking hours.

Q. How does the speaker begin the lecture?

Answer Key Ⓐ

🎧 Practice 3

Listening Script

W: James, thank you for coming on such short <u>notice</u>.

M: No problem, Ms. Harris. I was just downstairs when you called me.

W: Oh, okay then. Now, let me just get to the <u>point</u>. Are you working these days?

M: I <u>wish I were</u>. But, it's hard to find a part-time job these days.

W: Then, how would you like to work in my research lab... um... say, ten hours a week?

M: Really? That would be great! Um, but... what would I be <u>doing</u>?

W: Well, just basic <u>maintenance</u> of the lab. Nothing you can't <u>handle</u> I suppose.

M: Sure. I'm <u>flattered</u> that you've even considered me for this job.

W: Well, the <u>pleasure</u> is mine.

Q. Why did the woman ask the man to see her?

Answer Key Ⓑ

Part II

🎧 Practice 4

Listening Script

Prof(M): There's an interesting device recently developed by the National Space Biomedical Research Institute. It's a wearable and non-invasive sensory device that can be put on the surface of human skin. And this is how it works. Near-infrared light from the sensor penetrates through the skin and through the fat and into the muscle. Then light is absorbed by small blood vessels and the machine connected to the sensor will analyze the information in the person's blood. Sounds like a device from a spy movie, doesn't it? It was initially developed to measure the metabolic rates of astronauts, and the level of oxygen consumption. Now, why is this important information? Well, the astronauts need to know their metabolic rates in order to plan their activities and make sure that they don't run out of oxygen. Apparently, this sensor can be an effective device for medical care as well. Data from this skin sensor could also be used for hospital patients to make sure the patient is getting an appropriate treatment. Depending on the degree of the patient status, the information from the sensor can help avoid life threatening situations.

Q1. What is the main topic of the lecture?

Q2. Why do astronauts need to know their metabolic rate?

Q3. How does the speaker organize the lecture?

Answer Key

A Q1. Ⓑ   Q2. Ⓒ   Q3. Ⓐ

B 1. **device**   2. **skin**   3. **blood**   4. **metabolic**
   5. **oxygen**   6. **run out**   7. **treatment**   8. **avoid**

🎧 Practice 5

Listening Script

Prof(M): I'm sure many of you have a cell phone in your pocket right now. These days, a cell phone surely is one of the essential personal items we carry, isn't it? Most cell phone owners carry his or her phone everyday and just about everywhere they go all day long. Now, these familiar devices and their owners can be a new tool for experimental studies as mobile sensors. You see, cell phones are like little computers that constantly collect information about you. You can even upload that information from your phone onto a server on the Internet. Things like the pictures you took, phone numbers, schedules and so on. And when this information is put into context and arranged appropriately, it can tell you quite a lot about your lifestyle. For example, the data collected from your cell phone can tell you about the amount of pollution you create and how much you are exposed to it throughout the day. In fact, it's a new and interesting way to measure your choices in your daily life. At the same time, it can also help you make smart changes to live a more environmentally sustainable life. And for a scientist like me, cell phone surveys are effective and accurate ways to study how people move and live in urban settings.

Q1. What does the speaker mainly discuss?

Q2. Why does the speaker mention computers?

Q3. The speaker describes examples of the information that cell phones can collect about you. Check if each of the following is mentioned or not. Put a check mark in the correct box.

Answer Key

A Q1. Ⓑ   Q2. Ⓐ   Q3. **Mentioned:** Ⓐ, Ⓒ
   Not mentioned: Ⓑ, Ⓓ

B 1. **personal**   2. **tool**   3. **collect**
   4. **lifestyle**   5. **create**   6. **choices**
   7. **sustainable**   8. **urban**

🎧 Practice 6

Listening Script

M: Hello, Emily. I wanted to see you because you seemed out of focus in the class these days.

W: Um... yeah, I was a bit lost especially for the last few sessions.

M: Well, it isn't like you. You're usually one of the most energetic students.

W: I'm sorry. It's just that I can't really grasp the concept of quantum mechanics. I read the textbook and reviewed the class notes, but I still don't understand it.

M: I see. Then, why didn't you come and see me after the class?

W: I would've if I had the time. But, I always have to run to my part-time work right after the class.

M: Well, Emily, I have office hours on Thursdays for students like you. You know that, right?

W: I know. But, I have to work all day on Thursdays. So....

M: Hmm... then, why don't you just e-mail me? I'll be happy to answer your questions.

W: I will try to do that from now on. And, thank you so much for your concern.

M: Well, I just want to make sure that no students are lost in my classroom.

Q1. Why does the man want to see the woman?

Q2. What does the man offer to do for the woman?

Answer Key

A Q1. Ⓒ Q2. Ⓐ

B 1. **focus**   2. **understand**   3. **Office hours**
   4. **Work**   5. **E-mail**

Test 1

Listening Script

Listen to part of a lecture in a space science class.

Prof(W): Astronauts on space missions usually don't have much choice in eating. They are expected to eat mostly frozen or vacuum dried food packed in special plastic wrapping. Scientists and chefs try to develop a more interesting menu like vacuum-dried tomato soup, or frozen dried fruit flakes. Well, I don't know about you, but they surely wouldn't be my idea of an appetizing meal. However, eating on Mars might be more enjoyable for astronauts and even somewhat similar to an ordinary meal on Earth. According to NASA, future astronauts will be able to grow crops and cook their own vegetarian meals on missions to Mars. NASA recently conducted a research project in the Arctic to simulate the experience of living on Mars for 100 days. The space crew was able to have the same ingredients for food and guess what, a small indoor garden! Fascinating, isn't it? Now, one of the crew actually came up with a food recipe called TVP sweet and sour meatballs. It is actually textured vegetable protein shaped in balls, kind of like meatballs, and fried with teriyaki sauce. She had it over fried rice and added some sprouts from the indoor garden. Pretty fancy for a space meal, don't you think? By the way, it turns out that the crew of astronauts in the project had something more important than the taste of food. It was the social aspect of eating together. During the simulation, they gathered together to eat and talk every night. They enjoyed that they could still have some of the normal and everyday human life experiences in an unfamiliar setting, such as a simulated environment on Mars.

Now, get ready to answer the questions.

Q1. What does the speaker mainly discuss?

Q2. How does the speaker begin his lecture?

Q3. What did NASA's research project in the Arctic try to experiment?

Q4. What is the speaker's attitude toward vacuum or frozen dried food?

Q5. What did the astronauts in the project find to be important?

Answer Key

Q1. Ⓐ Q2. Ⓐ Q3. Ⓒ Q4. Ⓓ Q5. Ⓒ

Test 2

Listening Script

Listen to part of a discussion in an environment class.

Prof(M): Okay, so far, we've talked about the importance of recycling. Before we move on to discuss more effective ways to recycle, does anyone have any questions?

W: Yes. I just want to know why certain items can be recycled and others are not?

Prof(M): That's a good question. Ideally, everything, in other words, any material could be recycled. Practically, however, there are some materials that have been changed so much while going through their manufacturing process. In such cases, those materials become very difficult to recycle. For example, food cans and soda cans are easy to recycle. But how about car tires? They are made of rubber which is chemically processed. So they are nearly impossible to recycle into new rubber products.

W: How about computers? They have a lot of metal and plastic parts. Why can't we recycle computers?

Prof(M): Well, you're right. Computers have a lot of recyclable parts, but the problem is that they are made of so many different materials. Therefore, they are hard to take apart for recycling. And even though some parts actually get recycled, the process of recycling sometimes can be more expensive than buying new parts.

W: So, if you can recycle a material for less than the cost of using a new material, then it would be considered recyclable. Is that it?

Prof(M): That would be one thing. And it's pretty simple. If recycling a material is difficult and more expensive than a new material, people won't want to use it. However, we should not dismiss the environmental benefits of recycling besides the economic cost. One good example would be recycling papers. You see, in some parts of the world, it may be cheaper to print a book on new paper than to use recycled paper. However, continuous logging of trees to make new paper will reduce the number of trees. This of course will hurt the environment eventually. Then, even though it is more costly for now, it might be more beneficial to use recycled paper in the long run.

Now, get ready to answer the questions.

Q1. What is the main topic of the discussion?

Q2. How does the professor begin the discussion?

Q3. Why does the professor say that computers are difficult to recycle?

Q4. Which of the following is mentioned as easily recyclable?

Q5. According to the discussion, what should be considered with regards to recycling? Click on 2 answers.

Answer Key

Q1. Ⓑ   Q2. Ⓐ   Q3. Ⓒ   Q4. Ⓑ   Q5. Ⓐ, Ⓑ

Test 3

Listening Script

Listen to a conversation between a student and a teacher.

M: Hi, Linda. Good to see you again. How have you been?

W: Great, Mr. Adrienne, but I really miss your French class from last semester.

M: Well, I also miss having you in my classroom as well. So, what's up?

W: Um, I'm applying for the one year exchange student program to France.

M: Oh, that's exciting! You'll love studying in France.

W: Well, I'm sure I would if I could go.

M: I know that the competition is quite high. But, hey, you were one of my best students in my French class.

W: Well, but I'm afraid that my other grades may not be high enough.

M: *Hey, you never know. So, give yourself a chance.*

W: I will. So, I was just wondering if you could review my French essay for the application. It's quite short, just one page.

M: Well, sure, that shouldn't be too hard. Do you have it with you?

W: Uh, no. I'm still working on it but I could email it to you by this afternoon. I thought I should check with you first.

M: Okay, you know my email address, right? I'll run through it tonight.

W: Sure. Thank you so much, Mr. Adrienne. This means a lot to me.

M: No problem. I'm glad to be a help.

Now, get ready to answer the questions.

Q1. Why does the woman come to see the man?

Q2. What can be said about the man?

Q3. Why does the man say this: "Hey, you never know. So, give yourself a chance."

Q4. What is the woman concerned about in applying for the exchange program?

Answer Key

Q1. Ⓓ   Q2. Ⓑ   Q3. Ⓐ   Q4. Ⓐ

Listening Helper

Answer Key

A 1. **threat**   2. **detected**   3. **refreshed**
4. **flattered**   5. **consumption**   6. **exposed**
7. **sustainable**   8. **lost**   9. **vacuum**
10. **ingredients**

B 1. **dismiss,** Ⓐ   2. **overloaded,** Ⓒ
3. **contrary,** Ⓑ   4. **handle,** Ⓒ
5. **penetrates,** Ⓒ   6. **context,** Ⓐ
7. **grasp,** Ⓑ   8. **appetizing,** Ⓒ
9. **run through,** Ⓐ   10. **invasive,** Ⓒ

Unit 4 | Academic Lectures: Minds and Behaviors | Conversations

Practices

Warm Up

Answer Key

1. Social, human
2. Hyenas, giggles
3. trained, remember
4. adventures, life
5. gestures
6. memory, rainforest

Part I

Practice 1

Listening Script

Prof(W): One of the most important features that <u>defines</u> humans would be social interaction. Many anthropologists say that how we <u>learn</u> to interact with each other or, our social intelligence enabled humans to be <u>unique</u> among other species. I would go <u>further</u> to say that it was perhaps a critical <u>element</u> in our evolution. Looking at fossil records and other archeological <u>evidence</u> of behavior, it seems that the size of human brain <u>increased</u> about 250 percent in less than 3 million years. I believe that humans required large brains <u>in order to</u> work their ways in different social situations and <u>groups</u>. I mean, there were competition, cooperation and other types of interactions that we had to deal with other humans. So, naturally, social interaction and social intelligence became more and more important <u>throughout</u> human evolution. The anthropologists go so far as to say that it was social intelligence that <u>brought</u> humans to evolutionary success.

Q. What can be inferred about the size of human brain?

Answer Key Ⓐ

Practice 2

Listening Script

Prof(M): Hyena language can be an <u>intriguing</u> subject to study. *Some of you might wonder if hyenas even have a language. Then, I'd say that you are <u>in for</u> a surprise.* You see, hyenas, particularly the spotted ones are <u>highly</u> social animals. And, they have a wide range of <u>vocal</u> communication including the giggles and groans. Actually, hyenas are quite <u>well known</u> for their unusual giggles, but for now, let's <u>stick to</u> their groans. After extensive research, experts <u>concluded</u> that hyenas make two types of groans. One is a low-pitched and monotonous groan. It usually gives an <u>aggressive</u> message such as telling others to stay away from the <u>meat</u> it has discovered. The other type of groan <u>varies</u> between high and low pitches sounding almost like music. This kind of groan is heard a lot when a mother hyena is <u>caring</u> for her cubs. It probably works as a way to reassure and <u>comfort</u> cubs.

Q. What does the speaker imply about hyenas when he says this: "Some of you might wonder if hyenas even have a language. Then, I'd say that you are in for a surprise."

Answer Key Ⓑ

🖳 Practice 3

Listening Script

M: Hello, my name is Jackson Hunt signing in for room 312. I'm here to pick up my keys.

W: Oh, you must be the new student. Do you have your luggage with you?

M: Actually, they're in my father's car. He's waiting in the parking lot to unload my stuff.

W: I see. Here's the key to your room and the magnetic card for the main entrance.

M: Is there any way I can come in through the back directly from the parking lot?

W: Sure, the magnetic key also works for the back door. You wouldn't want to drag your luggage all the way to the front door.

M: Oh, great. I was afraid I would have to do that.

Q. What can be inferred about the man?

Answer Key Ⓓ

Part II

🖳 Practice 4

Listening Script

Prof(W): How would you feel if I tell you that a five-year-old chimpanzee might be able to recall someone's phone number better than you? Well, there's a good chance it might be true. There was an interesting experiment comparing chimpanzees' memory to that of humans. Apparently chimpanzees can learn Arabic numbers from one to nine, you know, just like human children. The researchers trained three chimpanzees at the age of five to recognize the numbers one through nine. Then they had each chimp look at a computer monitor flashing Arabic numbers. The number appeared randomly on a touch screen and after less than a second, the numbers were covered by white squares. However, the chimps were able to remember the exact location of the numbers by touching them in correct numerical order. And guess what? The exact same experiment was done on a group of college students. While the college students struggled to recall the location of the numbers after five numbers, the chimps had no problem even with eight numbers!

Q1. What does the speaker mainly discuss?

Q2. How does the speaker organize the lecture?

Q3. What can be inferred about the college students in the experiment?

Answer Key

A Q1. Ⓓ Q2. Ⓐ Q3. Ⓒ

B 1. **recall**   2. **memory**   3. **flashed**

4. **location**   5. **order**   6. **struggled**

Practice 5

Listening Script

Prof(M): Some people look for adventures in life while others would rather enjoy a quiet and peaceful life. Now, ask yourself. Would you rather go bungee jumping, or stay home and read? If your decision is to go bungee jumping, that decision might already be wired into your brain. In other words, there's a part of your brain that makes you more of an adventure seeker than others. Let me back this up with a recent neuroscientific study. In this study, researchers tried to see the connection between the different parts of the brain that relate to personality. They know that seeking adventures like trying extreme sports or traveling is associated with two specific parts of the brain. In fact, these two parts connect new experiences to a sense of reward. What they tried to do was to see if this particular connection was stronger in some people than in others. At first, they asked people to fill out questionnaires to determine whether they were an adventure seeker. Then, they applied a brain imaging technique which examines neural fibers that connect different parts of the brain. And guess what? They found stronger fiber connections between the two specific parts of the brain for those who were adventure seekers. Therefore, this study shows that parts of our personality might be based on the structures and functions of our brains.

Q1. What is the main topic of the lecture?

Q2. According to the lecture, what can be inferred about the people who play extreme sports?

Q3. The speaker talks about a few processes involved in a neuroscientific study. Check if the following was involved in the processes. Put a check mark in the appropriate box.

Answer Key

A Q1. Ⓑ   Q2. Ⓑ   Q3. **Involved:** Ⓑ, Ⓒ
Not involved: Ⓐ, Ⓓ

B 1. **brain**   2. **associated**   3. **reward**
4. **personality**   5. **examines**   6. **stronger**
7. **structure**

Practice 6

Listening Script

M: Good morning. What can I do for you?

W: Hi, my name is Jessica Henson. I've been assigned to a residence room in the West House.

M: Let me see, Jessica Henson... oh yes, you'll be in room 4C in the West House.

W: That's right.

M: Okay, so, you're scheduled to move in next month, right?

W: Actually, that's why I'm here. Is it possible to come in a little early?

M: You mean you want to move in sometime this month?

W: Yes. I just found out that I need to move out of my apartment sooner than I thought.

M: Well, we usually don't allow early signing in. Um, but, how early are we talking about?

W: Um, maybe two weeks?

M: Hmm... let me see... oh, actually, one of our summer residents is checking out early. So, I guess we can make an exception for you.

W: Oh, Thank you so much. I really didn't want to burden my parents for two weeks.

M: I understand. However, you do have to pay for the extra two weeks of your residency.

W: Of course. That's not a problem.

Q1. Why does the student come to the office?

Q2. What can be inferred about the woman from the conversation?

Answer Key

A Q1. Ⓑ Q2. Ⓐ

B 1. **Assigned** 2. **apartment** 3. **Summer**
   4. **exception** 5. **parents**

Test 1

Listening Script

Listen to part of a talk given by a professor of early childhood education.

Prof(W): We often see children making spontaneous gestures. We know that it's just what children do. They sometimes point their fingers, raise their arms, or stomp their feet. Some children do it more than others and some of their gestures may be more meaningful than others. It's almost like children are trying to communicate something through their gestures. And, it's quite adorable to look at them in such motions... um, especially my two-year-old daughter. Anyway, most linguists agree that children with parents who speak to them more are likely to have a higher vocabulary. However, a new research shows that gesturing also affects vocabulary and the effect of gesturing can be even greater than the effect of speech. *So, we know that children gesturing is not just cute stuff.* Susan Goldin-Meadow is a psychologist and professor at the University of Chicago. She says that children are perfectly capable of picking up gestures from adults. She also says that this ability can actually help them learn language better. Her new research suggests that 14-month-old children who gesture more are likely to have a higher vocabulary by the time they enter kindergarten. Researchers also tested the children's vocabulary around the time they start primary school. They found that children who had gestured more at a younger age achieved significantly higher scores on vocabulary tests. This doesn't mean that gesturing itself causes a higher vocabulary. However, it could mean that gesturing and vocabulary acquisition are closely linked with each other. The researchers suggest that gesturing may encourage children to think more creatively by bringing out new ideas. It can also help them think more clearly by connecting their gestures with specific words.

Now, get ready to answer the questions.

Q1. What does the speaker mainly discuss?

Q2. Which of the following would affect children's vocabulary? Click on 2 answers.

Q3. What do the researchers suggest gesturing does for children?

Q4. What does the speaker imply when she says this:
"So, we know that children gesturing is not just cute stuff."

Q5. What is the speaker's point about children's gesturing and vocabulary acquisition?

Answer Key

Q1. Ⓐ   Q2. Ⓐ, Ⓑ   Q3. Ⓓ
Q4. Ⓑ   Q5. Ⓓ

Test 2

Listening Script

Listen to part of a lecture in a behavioral science class.

Prof(M): Many of you probably heard about chimpanzees having good memories. Now, how about other animals? Are there other animals that also have good memories? Well, the answer is yes and one that I'd like to talk about today is elephants. Elephants are known to have incredible memories. You see, when you think about where elephants live, it is not that surprising. They live in the rainforest which is one of the most complicated natural environments on our planet. However, elephants somehow know where fruit trees are and where else to go to get their food. A rainforest is not only a complicated habitat but also a huge place. The size of a rainforest can easily extend to a thousand square miles. Can you imagine getting around such a large environment without getting lost? It surely would involve a lot of memory, wouldn't it? Now, it's not just the life in the jungle that requires elephants to have good memories, but also their social lives. In fact, it is their social setting that makes their memory more special and impressive. You see, elephants are known to live in groups of 500 to 1,000. Researchers found out that an elephant can distinguish every single one of the members in the group. Oh, by the way, elephants have the largest brain among land animals and it can weigh up to 5 kilograms. Well, it certainly makes sense for them to have such a large brain in order to store all that complicated memory.

Now, get ready to answer the questions.

Q1. What is the main topic of the lecture?

Q2. How does the speaker describe the environment of a rainforest? Click on 2 answers.

Q3. Which of the following requires elephants to have good memories? Click on 2 answers.

Q4. What does the speaker imply about the large brain size of elephants?

Q5. According to the speaker, what is impressive about the social settings of elephants?

Answer Key

Q1. Ⓑ   Q2. Ⓑ, Ⓓ   Q3. Ⓐ, Ⓒ   Q4. Ⓐ
Q5. Ⓐ

Test 3

Listening Script

Listen to part of a conversation between two people in a housing office.

W: Hi, can I help you?

M: Yes. I'm in room 209 and I'm having some problems in my room. I think someone should come and take a look.

W: What kind of problems?

M: Well, the first thing is my window. For some reason, it got stuck last night and wouldn't close.

W: *Did you try calling the custodian on duty?*

M: *I did, but had no luck in getting him.* So, I had to sleep with my window open last night.

W: Oh, I'm sorry to hear that. I hope you didn't catch a cold or anything.

M: I sure hope not.

W: Were you at least able to use the radiator to heat up your room?

M: Actually, that's another reason why I'm here. My radiator is also doing something funny.

W: What do you mean 'funny?' What does it do?

M: When I turn it on, it makes a really loud noise.

W: *Well, you know, this is an old building. So, it usually makes some noise.*

M: *But, it also leaks rusty water, quite a lot actually.*

W: *It does? Hmm, that doesn't sound too good.*

M: Do you think it can be fixed today? I heard it's going to be really cold again tonight.

W: Well, I'll send our maintenance staff right away and have a look at your room.

M: Okay then, thank you.

Now, get ready to answer the questions.

Q1. Why does the man come to the office?

Q2. Why did the man sleep with his window open last night?

Q3. Listen again to part of the conversation. Then answer the question.

W: Well, you know, this is an old building. So, it usually makes some noise.

M: But, it also leaks rusty water, quite a lot actually.

W: It does? Hmm, that doesn't sound too good.

> What does the woman imply when she says this:
> "Hmm, that doesn't sound too good."

Q4. Listen again to part of the conversation. Then answer the question.

W: Did you try calling the custodian on duty?

M: I did, but had no luck in getting him.

> What can be inferred from this?

Answer Key

Q1. Ⓑ Q2. Ⓑ Q3. Ⓐ Q4. Ⓓ

Listening Helper

Answer Key

A 1. **cooperation** 2. **stick to** 3. **monotonous**
   4. **randomly** 5. **recall** 6. **be wired into**
   7. **residency** 8. **reassure** 9. **luck**
   10. **acquisition**

B 1. **defines,** Ⓐ 2. **unload,** Ⓐ 3. **drag,** Ⓑ
   4. **fill out,** Ⓑ 5. **burden,** Ⓑ 6. **pick up,** Ⓑ
   7. **store,** Ⓑ 8. **got stuck,** Ⓐ
   9. **custodian,** Ⓐ 10. **spontaneous,** Ⓑ

Unit 5 | Academic Lectures: Nature and Society
Conversations

Practices

Warm Up

Answer Key

1. animals, milk
2. fresh water
3. longer, healthier
4. early, fire
5. borders
6. land, crops

Part I

Practice 1
Listening Script

Prof(W): Humans have been able to respond to changes in the environment, both genetically and uh, culturally. The fact that we have skillful fingers and binocular vision is the evidence of our genetic evolution. We also went through cultural evolution by learning how to farm, and how to write and record history. Furthermore, we've changed our own environment then evolved as well in response to those changes. Think about the domestication of wild animals. When some people began taming animals, they also began drinking milk. This eventually changed our body to handle lactose from milk. *Now, let's look at this from a different perspective.* How about the future? Well, I believe that it's our ability to adapt to the changes in the environment that may save us in the future. For example, instead of burning fossil fuels for energy, we could try to adapt to alternative energy sources such as solar-hydrogen energy.

Q. What does the speaker mean when she says this:
"Now, let's look at this from a different perspective."

Answer Key

Practice 2
Listening Script

Prof(M): There is a growing concern about the supply of fresh water worldwide. Many of us living in wealthier nations have no difficulty getting safe drinking water. So, we take our access to fresh water for granted and don't realize how this could be a serious problem in other parts of the world. In fact, there are more than a billion people around the world that don't have access to fresh water, not to mention drinking water. Now, the number gets more outrageous when we count people who don't have access to sufficient sanitation services. *That would be 2.5 billion people which means about 40 percent of the world's population! Think about that!* In fact, the lack of sanitation service is quite critical because that could lead to water-related diseases. And as you're already well aware, water-related diseases lead to a large number of deaths of mostly young children.

Q. Listen again to part of the lecture. Then answer the question.

Prof(M): That would be 2.5 billion people which means about 40 percent of the world's population! Think about that!

Why does the speaker say this: "Think about that!"

Answer Key Ⓐ

Practice 3
Listening Script

W: Hey, Jude. Have you decided who you're going to vote for the student president?

M: Well, to tell you the truth, I don't even know who's running for the position.

W: Are you serious? You should pay more attention to what's going on.

M: I'm just not into things like that. *It's just not my cup of tea.*

W: But, electing the student president is quite important. It can change our campus life depending on who gets elected.

M: I suppose. I guess I'm just too lazy to study the campaign issues for the election.

W: Come on, where's your school spirit? At least read the campaign posters for each candidate.

M: All right. You have a point. I'll check them out.

Q. What does the man mean when he says this:
"It's just not my cup of tea."

Answer Key Ⓓ

Part II

Practice 4
Listening Script

Prof(W): Good morning. Um, I read an interesting article this morning related to what we've been talking about these last few weeks. *So, maybe I should fill you in on the article first and resume our discussion.* The article talks about the report made by the United Nations on global population. According to this report, more than one out of five people on Earth will be over the age of sixty by 2050. This means that the number of people who are sixty and over is going to almost triple in about four decades. That's a big increase in a relatively short period of time. So, why is this a big concern? Well, it is clear that the world has to adapt to an ageing population. And...

the main concern is not so much about societal adaptation, but rather, economic adaptation. The key word here is the workforce. Because people live longer and remain healthier, older people are expected to stay in the workforce longer. Then, there may not be enough jobs left for young people to take. So, there is going to be a lot of unemployment which will stagnate the world's economy as a result.

Q1. What is the main topic of the lecture?

Q2. According to the lecture, what is expected of older people?

Q3. What does the speaker mean when she says this:
"So, maybe I should fill you in on the article first and resume our discussion."

Answer Key

A Q1. B   Q2. D   Q3. A

B 1. **global**   2. **sixty**   3. **ageing**
   4. **workforce**   5. **stay**   6. **young**
   7. **stagnation**

Practice 5

Listening Script

Prof(M): There have been a number of 'the great leap forward' in human history. In the beginning, our culture evolved at a very slow pace. The same kind of primary stone tools were used for hundreds of thousands of years. Then, there was a kind of a cultural revolution where we began using more advanced tools. We also began to sew clothes with fine needles and do cave paintings. Then more dramatic changes in human culture followed. *Nevertheless, many of these great leaps forward boil down to two very dramatic events.* And anthropologists estimate that the first great leap forward happened between 50 and 100 thousand years ago. Now, what initiated this first great leap forward? Well, it was of course the discovery and the use of fire. By using fire, we were able to dominate the environment and began developing human culture. Now, the second and perhaps the biggest step forward in human history happened about ten thousand years ago. It was when we began practicing agriculture. Agriculture made it possible for humans to grow enough food to settle in one place and start our civilization. By learning how to farm and settle down, we became increasingly smart and social animals. Without agriculture, we wouldn't be too different from other large mammals living on the planet.

Q1. What does the speaker mainly discuss?

Q2. What does the speaker mean when he says this:
"Nevertheless, many of these great leaps forward boil down to two very dramatic events."

Q3. The speaker talks about the outcome of agriculture on humans. Check if the following has been mentioned as one of the outcomes or not. Put a check mark in the appropriate box.

Answer Key

A Q1. C   Q2. C   Q3. **Mentioned:** A, C, D
   Not mentioned: B, E

B 1. **slowly**   2. **tools**   3. **Discovery**   4. **culture**
   5. **biggest**   6. **food**   7. **increasingly**

🔊 Practice 6

Listening Script

W: Hello. Can I help you?

M: Yes, please. I'm here to sign up for the campus half marathon this weekend.

W: Okay, did you bring the sign-up sheet?

M: Yes, here you go. And... how much is the registration fee?

W: It's 5 dollars. You can give it to me now, or pay at the reception desk on Saturday.

M: Oh, really? What's the difference?

W: Well, if you pay now, in other words, if you pre-register, you get a free t-shirt and water bottles.

M: Oh, free souvenirs! *Well, there's no reason not to do it then*.

W: But, you should keep in mind that the registration fee is not refundable. In other words, even if you don't show up for the race you won't get your money back.

M: Yes, of course. I understand. And I know that I'll definitely be there on Saturday.

W: Okay, good. Now, let me see... so, your name is Jerry Parker, right?

M: Uh-huh.

W: All right, Jerry, wait here and I'll bring the t-shirt and the bottles for you.

M: Sure. Thanks.

Q1. Why does the man come to the office?

Q2. What does the woman say about pre-registration?

Q3. What does the man mean when he says this:
"Well, there's no reason not to do it then."

Answer Key

A Q1. Ⓓ Q2. Ⓑ Q3. Ⓐ

B 1. **half** 2. **sign-up** 3. **fee** 4. **souvenirs**
   5. **showing up** 6. **definitely**

Test 1

Listening Script

Listen to part of a lecture in a sociology class.

Prof(W): Do you know any friend or relative who is living abroad? I don't think it is uncommon to find someone or a family member around us who has migrated to other countries. Every year, a growing number of people have been crossing their country's borders for a better lifestyle or work opportunities. So, let's take some time to look at this increasing trend of migration around the world. Now, did you know that about 3% of the entire world population is living abroad? *So, nearly 200 million people in the world are currently living outside their home country. And given the continuing trend of globalization, this number is less likely to get smaller or remain the same.* Oh, just to clarify... what I mean by home country is the country in which people were born. It seems that people feel much less limited by the boundaries of countries compared to twenty or thirty years ago. Nowadays, people have more information and ideas about living abroad. Therefore, many people have recognized that they might be able to do better elsewhere instead of staying in their home country. One thing we should notice is that most international migration is to a few wealthy countries such as the United States, Canada, and Australia. *Also, the bigger the population of the destination country, the larger the number of the immigrants. Um... actually, let me come back to this shortly.* Now, it is important to know just how many people are moving where, especially, the destination countries. These countries need to have a good picture of its future demographic changes to plan policies for critical issues... uh..., such as pension, schools, jobs, health care, and so on. So, when you look at the whole picture, migration affects not only the lives of people who are crossing the borders, but all people in the communities into which people migrate.

Now, get ready to answer the questions.

Q1. What does the speaker mainly discuss?

Q2. Listen again to part of the lecture. Then answer the question.

Prof(W): So, nearly 200 million people in the world are currently living outside their home country. And given the continuing trend of globalization, this number is less likely to get smaller or remain the same.

What does the speaker imply when she says this:
"And given the continuing trend of globalization, this number is less likely to get smaller or remain the same."

Q3. According to the speaker, what motivates people to migrate to other countries? Click on 2 answers.

Q4. Listen again to part of the lecture. Then answer the question.

Prof(W): Also, the bigger the population of the destination country, the larger the number of the immigrants. Um... actually, let me come back to this shortly.

What does the speaker mean when she says this:
"Um... actually, let me come back to this shortly."

Q5. Why is it important for the destination countries to know the trend of immigration?

Answer Key

Q1. Ⓑ   Q2. Ⓐ   Q3. Ⓐ, Ⓒ   Q4. Ⓒ
Q5. Ⓑ

Test 2

Listening Script

Listen to part of a talk given by an economics professor.

Prof(M): I'd like to talk about an age-old system called sharecropping which existed since ancient Egypt. When people didn't own any land to grow their crops, they often became sharecroppers. Sharecroppers are the people who farm land that was owned by somebody else, usually a rich man. So instead of renting the land, the crop harvested from the land was shared between the sharecropper and the landowner. However, the sharecropper would do all the work of plowing the land, planting the seeds, weeding and harvesting. After the crop was harvested, the sharecropper usually kept half of it and the landowner got the other half. So, I'm sure that not all sharecroppers were happy about that deal. Anyway, after the Civil War in the United States, many freed black slaves began working as sharecroppers in the cotton fields. It was better than working for wages because they would still be taking orders from the white employer. And working as sharecroppers, black people hoped that they would be able to buy their own cotton field someday. So, being a sharecropper was certainly better than being enslaved. *It is needless to say*. However, most of them were still poor since a large portion of the harvest had to go to the landowner. A lot of them couldn't even buy enough food and clothes. Even if they saved up enough money, it was difficult for them to buy land because mostly white landowners were reluctant to sell their land to black people. Eventually, a lot of sharecroppers ended up borrowing money from the landowner and soon they were permanently in debt. They couldn't even give up sharecropping and leave the land even if they wanted to because of the debt. Therefore, in many cases, sharecropping ended up being another form of slavery for many black people.

Now, get ready to answer the questions.

Q1. What is the main topic of the lecture?

Q2. What does the speaker imply about sharecropping?

Q3. What does the speaker mean when he says this:
"It is needless to say."

Q4. What are the sharecroppers expected to do? Click on 2 answers.

Q5. Why couldn't the freed black slaves buy their own cotton fields? Click on 2 answers.

Answer Key

Q1. Ⓐ Q2. Ⓒ Q3. Ⓒ Q4. Ⓐ, Ⓓ
Q5. Ⓐ, Ⓒ

Test 3

Listening Script

Listen to part of a conversation in a school office.

W: May I help you?

M: Yes, I was trying to sign up for the field trip to the art gallery.

W: You were trying to do that on the website?

M: Yes, but it won't allow me to sign up saying that I've already been on the last field trip.

W: Well, students are allowed only one trip per semester in case you didn't know.

M: You see, I signed up for the last trip but I couldn't go because I got injured playing soccer the night before.

W: Did you call our office and give a cancellation notice?

M: I'm afraid I could not. I was really in bad shape the next day.

W: Well, that's why. As far as the record goes, you've already completed one trip.

M: But, I didn't go.

W: *I'm sorry, but you really should've called to cancel your registration.*

M: *Oh... this is really bad. I really need this trip to write the final report for my art course.*

W: Well....

M: Um... isn't there any way you can sign me up?

W: Hmm... I suppose you could show up right before the departure and ask. You know, try your luck.

M: What do you mean?

W: Well, there's a good chance that someone might fail to show up, just like you did.

M: Oh, I see. So, when that happens, I can fill in that spot.

W: Yeah. I'll make a note here with your name that you should be able to take over any cancellation.

M: Okay. I appreciate it.

W: That might be your best shot at this point.

M: Well, I guess that's better than no chance at all. Thanks anyway.

Now, get ready to answer the questions.

Q1. Why does the man come to the office?

Q2. Why does the man have a problem signing up for the field trip?

Q3. Why didn't the man go on his last field trip?

Q4. Listen again to part of the conversation. Then answer the question.

W: I'm sorry, but you really should've called to cancel your registration.

M: Oh... this is really bad. I really need this trip to write the final report for my art course.

  Why does the man say this:
  "Oh... this is really bad."

Answer Key

Q1. Ⓑ Q2. Ⓐ Q3. Ⓓ Q4. Ⓐ

Listening Helper

Answer Key

A 1. **binocular** 2. **domestication**
  3. **sanitation** 4. **candidate** 5. **stagnate**
  6. **initiated** 7. **migration** 8. **demographic**
  9. **reluctant** 10. **injured**

B 1. **worldwide,** Ⓑ 2. **into,** Ⓐ
  3. **fill, in on,** Ⓒ 4. **estimate,** Ⓐ
  5. **alternative,** Ⓑ 6. **keep in mind,** Ⓐ
  7. **shows up,** Ⓑ 8. **needless to say,** Ⓐ
  9. **in bad shape,** Ⓐ 10. **portion,** Ⓑ

Unit 6 | Academic Lectures: Arts and Culture
Conversations

Practices

Warm Up

Answer Key

1. **dance**

2. jumping, movements

3. common, colonists

4. outdoor

5. construction, natural

6. feast, salt

Part I

🔊 Practice 1

Listening Script

Prof(M): Many experts in music would <u>classify</u> 'ragtime', or 'ragtime jazz' to be <u>truly</u> American classic music. Ragtime is <u>indeed</u> an originally American music genre even though part of it <u>is rooted in</u> the rhythms of African music. Ragtime first began in the late 19th century as dance music in <u>slums</u> in cities like St. Louis and New Orleans. The popularity of ragtime reached its peak between 1897 and 1918, then it began to <u>die down</u>. Now, the most <u>distinct</u> feature of ragtime is its syncopated, or 'ragged' rhythm. This essentially means that weak beats are <u>stressed</u> instead of strong beats. ***Personally, I can listen to it for hours on end***. By the way, this syncopated beat enabled ragtime to be <u>regarded as</u> an American equivalent of minuets by Mozart or... Waltzes by Brahms. Interestingly, this true American classic also <u>influenced</u> a few European classical composers like... Igor Stravinsky and Claude Debussy.

Q. What can be said about the speaker and ragtime jazz when he says this: "Personally, I can listen to it for hours on end."

Answer Key

🔊 Practice 2

Listening Script

Prof(W): (enthusiastically) ***Okay, Isadora Duncan... let's see... where should I begin...*** I mean, she was a woman of many <u>titles</u>; she was a dancer, an adventurer, a poet, a radical thinker and so <u>many more</u>. However, she is most <u>prominently</u> known as a theorist of dance as well as a talented dancer. As a theorist of dance, she developed free and <u>natural</u> movements that were considered quite radical <u>in her time</u>. These movements were <u>inspired by</u> the classical Greek art, folk dances, social dances as well as nature. She also <u>incorporated</u> ideas from the new American athleticism and <u>included</u> skipping, running, jumping and leaping. As a dancer, she was famous for her <u>free-flowing</u> costumes and bare feet <u>during</u> performances. Her movements were simple <u>yet</u> deep with a new kind of <u>vitality</u>. With her revolutionary ideas and passion, she was able to <u>restore</u> dance to a high place <u>among</u> other forms of art and became a <u>pioneer</u> of today's modern dance.

Q. What is the speaker's attitude when she says this:
"Okay, Isadora Duncan... let's see... where should I begin..."

Answer Key

Script & Answer Keys •• 33

Practice 3
Listening Script

W: Hi, I'd like to <u>drop off</u> these books.

M: Sure. Uh... you know what? Some of these books are <u>overdue</u> and you <u>owe</u> us 5 dollars.

W: *No way!* I thought they were all <u>due</u> today.

M: Well, some are. But these three <u>should've been</u> returned two weeks ago.

W: Hmm, well, do I pay the overdue charge here?

M: Um, no. You need to go downstairs to the <u>accounting</u> office. They'll <u>take care of</u> it for you.

W: Okay. I can't believe I got <u>mixed up</u> with the due dates.

M: Well, you know, it happens.

Q. What can be said about the woman when she says this:
"No way!"

Answer Key   Ⓓ

Part II

Practice 4
Listening Script

Prof(W): One of the more traditional ways of building a roof is called thatching. To make a thatched roof, the wooden skeleton of a roof is covered with reeds or straw. You don't really see thatched roofs in the United States these days. But, in the 17th century, they were quite common among the colonists. Then, other roofing materials such as woods, stone or clay tiles became popular and eventually replaced thatched roofs. Actually, it's too bad that most people today do not realize the great benefits of a thatched roof. One of the benefits is its strength. You see, a thatched roof is made of straw and reeds. Really, nothing too fancy or hi-tech. But they are very flexible so they bend in case of strong winds without breaking like other materials. Therefore, the roof can survive the wind. Another benefit of a thatched roof is its long lifespan. An average lifespan of a thatched roof is about sixty years and it can last up to a hundred. Also, a thatched roof has a high insulative value because it keeps the house cool in the summer and warm in the winter. *Well, aren't these good enough reasons why a thatched roof should really make a comeback?*

Q1. What does the speaker mainly discuss?

Q2. What is the speaker's attitude toward a thatched roof when she says this:
"Well, aren't these good enough reasons why a thatched roof should really make a comeback?"

Q3. Which of the following is mentioned as the benefits of a thatched roof? Click on 2 answers.

Answer Key
A Q1. Ⓓ   Q2. Ⓐ   Q3. Ⓑ , Ⓓ
B 1. **Wooden**   2. **replaced**   3. **flexible**
   4. **wind**   5. **lifespan**   6. **insulative**

Practice 5

Listening Script

Prof(M): When it comes to impressionism, there are a few common misunderstandings. Let me just mention a couple of them. Um..., the first misconception is that Impressionists are 'outdoor' painters. You see, they certainly painted a great deal of landscapes and popularized them. However, the Impressionists did not paint all their work outdoors. In fact, most of them spent more time in their indoor studios to complete their work. (firmly) *Then, we really should not label them outdoor painters, should we?* Anyway, the second misconception is that the Impressionists were disliked by the majority of art critics. Well, like any genre of artists, the Impressionists surely faced some harsh criticisms. *However, in truth, there was a much longer list of friendly critics and patrons of the Impressionists than the list of unkind ones.* Now, besides any misconceptions we might have, there is one truth about Impressionism that no one can argue. That is, Impressionism influenced generations of artists and spawned the multitude of art movements in Modern Art. Impressionism also influenced art viewers and critics and altered the way we look at art. In fact, we could probably go so far as to say that Impressionism changed art.

Q1. What is the main topic of the lecture?

Q2. What does the speaker imply when he says this:

" However, in truth, there was a much longer list of friendly critics and patrons of the Impressionists than the list of unkind ones."

Q3. What is the speaker's attitude when he says this:
"Then, we really should not label them outdoor painters, should we?"

Answer Key

A Q1. Ⓐ Q2. Ⓐ Q3. Ⓒ

B 1. **landscapes**   2. **disliked**   3. **friendly**
   4. **viewers**   5. **spawned**   6. **changed**

Practice 6

Listening Script

W: Hello. I need to find some video tapes for my psychology research.

M: Do you have the list?

W: Yes, here you go. I checked on the main search computer and it says all of them are currently available.

M: Um, yeah... hang on. Let me get them for you.

W: Thanks.

M: Okay, I have all three videos here. By the way, you do know that videos can't be checked out of the library, right?

W: Really? I didn't know that. Then, how can I look at them?

M: You can sign up for a viewing room upstairs. You're allowed to use it for two hours at a time.

W: Two hours? (anxiously) That won't give me enough time to look through all the videos. And my report is due tomorrow.

M: *Well, well, no need to panic.* You can extend your use of the room up to two more hours.

W: Oh, okay then. So, do I need to sign these out to take upstairs?

M: Yes, you do. Um, can I have your library card, please?

W: Of course. Here it is.

Q1. Why does the woman come to the library?

Q2. What is the man's attitude when he says this:
" Well, well, no need to panic."

Answer Key

A Q1. Ⓒ Q2. Ⓐ

B 1. **research** 2. **checked** 3. **viewing**
  4. **enough** 5. **due** 6. **extend**

Test 1

Listening Script

Listen to part of a lecture in an architecture class.

Prof(W): Good morning everyone. The focus of our discussion today is how to build and maintain an environmentally friendly architecture. Nowadays, architecture is rarely limited by the climate of the region. *You can build a handsome glass box high-rise whether its location is in Kuala Lumpur, Malaysia or Stockholm, Sweden. So, it's pretty much the same everywhere. However, planning and construction of traditional buildings had to be oriented by the natural environment. In fact, that helped to give the buildings their own regionally distinct charms unlike modern buildings.* From an environmentally friendly perspective, buildings that are hundreds or even thousands of years old were also more efficiently built than new buildings. They were designed to take advantage of the winds in the summer, or to make maximum use of the natural lighting for the winter. So, many architects are now trying to follow the idea of environmentally oriented architecture that can conserve energy. One particular example of that is the construction of a conference center in England inspired by a medieval Gothic cathedral. The architect and the constructors of this project tried to incorporate medieval technologies. Among those technologies were compressed earth walls using natural light and ventilation. In other words, they tried to build cutting-edge 21st century green architecture with medieval technologies. This was not only interesting but also highly efficient in terms of energy use. They say that this conference center took only 20% of the energy to build compared to a standard glass box building. And, what's more is that it now takes only less than 30% of the energy to maintain. Quite remarkable, isn't it? Well, buildings like this may seem to involve radical changes in the field of architecture. However, given our current crisis with energy, these changes might not be an option in the near future.

Now, get ready to answer the questions.

Q1. What is the main topic of the lecture?

Q2. Listen again to part of the lecture.

Then answer the question.

Prof(W): You can build a handsome glass box high-rise whether its location is in Kuala Lumpur, Malaysia or Stockholm, Sweden. So, it's pretty much the same everywhere. However, planning and construction of traditional buildings had to be oriented by the natural environment. In fact, that helped to give the buildings their own regionally distinct charms unlike modern buildings.

What is the speaker's attitude towards modern architecture?

Q3. Why does the speaker mention the conference center in England?

Q4. Which of the following represents a medieval feature in modern architecture?

Q5. What does the speaker imply about the field of architecture in the future?

Answer Key

Q1. Ⓑ   Q2. Ⓐ   Q3. Ⓓ   Q4. Ⓑ   Q5. Ⓑ

Test 2

Listening Script

Listen to part of a discussion about the culture of Medieval Europe.

Prof(M): In the Middle Ages in Europe, people didn't have too many choices in terms of food. Also, what people ate depended a lot on how rich they were. Actually, almost everybody was poor back then. So, what the poor people ate would be the most common diet of the time. Any guess on what it was? Well, it was barley. In fact, it seems that they ate barley every day, breakfast, lunch and dinner. People tried to be creative with their menu making barley into bread or pancakes, and sometimes into porridge or soup.

W: Still, that sounds quite boring. Didn't they have anything else to eat with it?

Prof(M): Sure. The poor people found other things to eat as much as they could. They grew carrots, onions, cabbage and garlic to make their barley meal a little more interesting and nutritious. Some grew herbs like basils or rosemary to flavor their food. They sometimes made cheese and gathered apples and mushrooms.

W: Um, did they have any kind of sweet food? *They didn't have sugar back then, did they?*

Prof(M): No, they didn't. But, they had honey to add a sweet taste.

W: How differently did the rich people eat?

Prof(M): The major difference would be eating wheat instead of barley. Wheat tasted better and they certainly had more choice of things to eat with their wheat bread. Oh, the rich people also had a wide range of meat in their diet such as pork, beef, lamb, deer and even rabbit. Another thing that the rich people were able to enjoy was spices like pepper and cinnamon. Spices were too expensive for the poor people because they had to come all the way from India.

W: I heard that salt was also very expensive in Medieval Europe.

Prof(M): That's right. In fact, during a big feast in a medieval castle, the salt would be on the table in a huge fancy container.

And only the rich people would sit near the salt so they could use it with their food. The poor people were seated further down the long table where it would be impossible for them to reach the salt. Have you ever heard people say that someone is "above the salt?" It means he or she is a rich person, and that's where the expression came from.

Now, get ready to answer the questions.

Q1. What is the main topic of the lecture?
Q2. What was the most common diet of the people in Medieval Europe?
Q3. What is the woman feeling when she says this:
"They didn't have sugar back then, did they?"
Q4. Which of the following was mentioned as a part of rich people's diet in Medieval Europe? Click on 2 answers.
Q5. Why does the professor mention the expression "above the salt" to the students?

Answer Key

Q1. Ⓑ Q2. Ⓐ Q3. Ⓐ Q4. Ⓐ, Ⓓ Q5. Ⓓ

Test 3

Listening Script

Listen to a conversation between two people on campus.

W: Hi, I'd like to purchase a meal plan here.

M: Okay, are you currently living on campus?

W: No, I'm not. Do I have to live in student housing to buy a meal plan?

M: Oh no. It's just that you can get a lower rate if you do.

W: *Really? Oh, well... I don't.*

M: Sorry. Anyway, how many meals do you plan to eat here per week?

W: Um, maybe about seven or eight times?

M: Well, in that case, maybe you should just buy meal tickets instead of a plan.

W: How are they different?

M: You can buy 10 meal tickets for 40 dollars. But, if you buy a meal plan, it will be 150 dollars for two weeks including weekends.

W: Oh, I see. So, if I don't eat here all the time, a meal plan would be a waste, is that it?

M: Yes. It makes more sense to buy the tickets.

W: I guess that's true... hmm....

M: By the way, if you live on campus, you're only allowed to buy the meal plan. So, maybe it's a good thing that you're a commuter.

W: Yeah? Maybe you're right then. Um, so... can I buy 2 sets?

M: You mean 20 meals?

W: Yes, please.

M: Sure. That will be 80 dollars. I also need to see your student ID.

Now, get ready to answer the questions.

Q1. What is the topic of the conversation?
Q2. What is the woman's attitude when she says this:

"Really? Oh, well... I don't."

Q3. Why is it a good thing that the woman is a commuter?

Q4. What does the woman decide to do?

Answer Key

Q1. Ⓓ   Q2. Ⓐ   Q3. Ⓑ   Q4. Ⓒ

Listening Helper

Answer Key

A 1. **prominently** 2. **overdue** 3. **skeleton**
   4. **majority** 5. **altered** 6. **conserve**
   7. **seated** 8. **feast** 9. **commuters**
   10. **panic**

B 1. **for hours on end,** Ⓑ 2. **earth,** Ⓒ
   3. **rooted,** Ⓐ 4. **incorporated,** Ⓐ
   5. **drop off,** Ⓑ 6. **bend,** Ⓒ
   7. **spawned,** Ⓐ 8. **extend,** Ⓐ
   9. **cutting-edge,** Ⓐ 10. **rate,** Ⓒ

Actual Test

Lecture: History

Listening Script

Listen to part of a discussion in a history class.

Prof(M): I'd like to talk about an interesting invention that changed the face of the American West in the late 19th century. Let me start by mentioning the name of a farmer from Illinois. *Does the name Joseph Glidden ring a bell for anyone?*

W: Was he the guy who invented a fencing wire with sharp barbs?

Prof(M): You're quite close. But, a barbed wire fence was first invented by Henry Rose, not Joseph Glidden. What he did was to come up with a new design for barbed wire.

W: Oh, I think I remember now. So, he was the one who started using two strands of wire instead of one, right?

Prof(M): Yes, that's right. The original invention by Henry Rose was a single stranded barbed wire. After Glidden saw this at an exhibition, he came up with a design that significantly improved on Rose's idea. He tried using two strands of wire twisted together to hold the barbed wires more firmly in place. So, it was Glidden's wire that soon got mass produced and by 1880, more than 80 million pounds of his barbed wire was sold. Now, who do you think bought these wires?

W: Wouldn't that be farmers from the Great Plains? I read from somewhere that there was a great increase in population in the Great Plains after the development of the railroad. So, the farmers felt the need to fence their property from intruders.

Prof(M): That's right. But, more importantly, farmers also needed the wire fence to protect their farms from the grazing herds of cattle and sheep. Back then, most of the cattle ranches were open which meant that cattle roamed around freely. And as the number of farms increased, farmers became annoyed with the roaming cattle and wanted to protect their property. So, this simple invention became a huge hit in the Great Plains. It was not only effective as fencing material, but also durable and best of all, highly affordable.

W: What did they use to build a fence before the barbed wire then?

Prof(M): Well, as you know, the plains didn't have a lot of trees. So, when a farmer wanted to build a fence, he had to buy heavy wooden rails from distant forests. The wooden rails were also very expensive because they had to be shipped by train or wagon. But with the initial idea of Henry Rose and the mass supply of Glidden's barbed wire, farmers could afford to build highly effective fences.

Now, get ready to answer the questions.

Q1. What is the main topic of the discussion?

Q2. Why did the farmers need to use barbed wire fences? Click on 2 answers.

Q3. The professor and the students discuss several events which happened in the late 19th century America. Put the following events into the correct order.

Q4. Which of the following describes the benefits of barbed wire? Click on 2 answers.

Q5. What does the professor mean when he says this:
"Does the name Joseph Glidden ring a bell for anyone?"

Answer Key
Q1. Ⓒ Q2. Ⓐ,Ⓒ Q3. Ⓑ-Ⓔ-Ⓐ-Ⓓ-Ⓒ
Q4. Ⓐ,Ⓓ Q5. Ⓓ

Lecture : Art

Listening Script

Listen to part of a lecture given in an art class.

Prof(M): When we talk about Dada or Dadaism, we understand it to be an artistic and literary movement. Ironically, the artists who were considered to be part of this movement would've denied that it was a movement. They probably did not even regard themselves as artists and their art to be art. That sounds a little puzzling, doesn't it? Well, to understand this irony, we need to look at the history of how Dada first began. As you might already know, Dada started in Europe around the time of World War I. When the war began to spread, a number of artists and intellectuals headed to Zurich in neutral Switzerland to get away from the horror of War. However, instead of feeling relieved and safe, these people were angry at the modern European society that allowed the war to happen. Then they began to protest by criticizing ideals such as nationalism, materialism and rationalism in any public forum. They thought these ideals had led society into a senseless direction and in fact, contributed to this pointless war. They eventually said that they didn't want to be a part of this society and its traditions, especially artistic traditions. They said that art, including all art throughout the world, has no meaning anymore. Then, they went on to proclaim themselves to be non-artists and whatever they created would be non-art. *In terms of public reaction to all this... well, the public was less than thrilled about it, I must say.* In fact, many people were even disgusted by their ideals and the work they created. However, the enthusiasm of the Dadaists began to spread all over Europe and New York City. Then, around the early 1920s, it was becoming more acceptable to mainstream artists and the enlightened public. Nevertheless, this is also when the 'true' movement of Dada began to dissolve and became less visible to the art world.

Now, get ready to answer the questions.

Q6. What is the main topic of the lecture?

Q7. Why did some artists and intellectuals go to Zurich, Switzerland?

Q8. According to the speaker, what is puzzling about the Dada movement?

Q9. What does the speaker imply about the public reaction when he says this:
"In terms of public reaction to all this... well, the public was less than thrilled about it, I must say."

Q10. What happened to the Dadaist in the early 1920s? Click on 2 answers.

Answer Key

Q6. Ⓓ   Q7. Ⓑ   Q8. Ⓒ   Q9. Ⓒ   Q10. Ⓑ,Ⓓ

Conversation

Listening Script

Listen to part of a conversation between a student and a professor during his office hour.

W: Professor Grant, may I talk with you for a minute?

M: Yes, Susan. What can I do for you?

W: Well, it's about the research paper that is due next Monday.

M: Yes, you are writing about nicotine and the brain, aren't you? How is it going?

W: It's coming along okay. I try to focus on how nicotine influences communication.

M: That sounds interesting. Oh, actually, I think Ted is working on a similar topic.

W: Is he? I didn't know that.

M: He is. Maybe you two should get together and share each other's references. Did you find enough books and articles?

W: *Well, I think I already have enough material to work with. If anything, I have more than I can handle at this point. So....*

M: Oh, all right, then.

W: It's just that... um, it's taking me a lot longer than I thought to finish the paper.

M: Sounds like you're asking for an extension. Right?

W: Um, yeah... if you could give me one.

M: Well, how much longer would you need?

W: Just a few more days.

M: Hmm... you know what? You've been pretty consistent with the quality of your work so far. So, I'll give you three more days. How's that?

W: That'll be great. Thank you.

M: *Well, not to put too much pressure on you, but your paper should deserve those extra days when I see it.*

W: Um, I'll do my best, sir.

Now, get ready to answer the questions.

Q11. What is the student's problem?

Q12. What does the professor suggest to the student?

Q13. What can be inferred about the student when she says this: "Well, I think I already have enough material to work with. If anything, I have more than I can handle at this point. So...."

Q14. What does the professor imply when he says this: "Well, not to put too much pressure on you, but your paper should deserve those extra days when I see it."

Answer Key

Q11. Ⓓ   Q12. Ⓐ   Q13. Ⓒ   Q14. Ⓑ

Lecture : Nutritional Science

Listening Script

Listen to part of a lecture in a nutritional science class.

Prof(M): As you know, the increase in greenhouse gas emissions is closely linked with the problem of climate change. Recently, I happened to come across a research result related to greenhouse gas emissions. Interestingly, it involves food we eat everyday, specifically, red meat and dairy products. Now, according to this research, eating less red meat and more chicken can help reduce greenhouse gas emissions. What the researchers tried to do was to figure out the effects that a product has on its environment over its lifetime. And they found that cows that produce beef and dairy products are considered environmentally expensive. First of all, When the bacteria in the cows' stomachs digest food, they produce methane. And methane is a very potent greenhouse gas, approximately 20 times stronger than carbon dioxide. Secondly, we should not dismiss the manure factor. You see, to produce one calorie of beef requires a lot more grain than to produce one calorie of chicken. It actually takes about twice as much grain to make a pound of beef from a cow as it does to make a pound of chicken. So, naturally, the amount of manure coming out of a cow happens to be a lot more per pound of meat than the amount coming out of chicken. And the real problem begins when this large amount of manure decomposes because it also releases very potent greenhouse gases. Now, it's not just grazing cows that causes greenhouse gas emissions. The researchers point out that producing food from cows generally creates far more greenhouse gas emissions than automobiles. To prove their point, they calculated the impact of giving up a day of red meat and dairy product each week. And guess what? It would have the same impact as driving about 1,500 miles less a year!

So..., maybe it's about time I go easy on the steaks and butter in my daily diet.

Now, get ready to answer the questions.

Q15. What is the main topic of the lecture?

Q16. How does the speaker organize his lecture?

Q17. According to the research, why are cows environmentally expensive?

Q18. What does the speaker imply about producing food from cows?

Q19. What can be said about the speaker when he says this: "So..., maybe it's about time I go easy on the steaks and butter in my daily diet."

Answer Key

Q15. Ⓓ   Q16. Ⓒ   Q17. Ⓐ   Q18. Ⓐ
Q19. Ⓒ

Lecture : Engineering

Listening Script

Listen to part of a lecture in an engineering class.

Prof(W): *Okay, if everyone is back from their break, let's start. We've got a long way to go and not much time left.* Before the break, we talked about some inventions inspired by the movement of animals. Now, I want to introduce another invention, but this time, inspired by a plant called venus flytrap. Although the venus flytrap is a plant, it acts like a cross between an animal and a machine. Like an animal, the plant kills and ingests the body of a fly to get the required nutrient from it. The way it captures its prey is quite interesting and works somewhat like a machine. When a fly lands on its leaf, the sensor inside the leaf is triggered making the leaf snap shut to capture the insect inside. There are no muscles in a flytrap's leaf because it's a plant, so, it's actually the cells of the plants that snap mechanically. Now, this mechanical property of the venus flytrap inspired researchers to design a number of material that acts similarly. Scientists from the University of Massachusetts tried imitating the snapping process by attaching two very thin layers of flexible material to each other. The layers were bonded in a way that there would be an internal pocket when they were closed. Then, using chemical signals or physical pressure, the scientists were able to make the material snap shut in an extremely short amount of time. This snapping happened almost automatically without any need to apply extra energy, well, just like the work of the plant's cells. The scientists say that this snapping process can also be triggered by heat or the level of humidity. Now, you must be wondering how this can be used in our daily lives. Well, for example, the technology of snapping surfaces can be applied in food packaging. It could work as sensors that react when the food in the package is spoiling. It could also be used to react in case the storage temperature is too high. This is just another way of learning from nature and coming up with something more functional to improve our lives.

Now, get ready to answer the questions.

Q20. What is the main topic of the lecture?

Q21. What causes the mechanical snap of a venus flytrap?

Q22. Which feature of the venus flytrap did scientists try to imitate?

Q23. Why does the speaker mention food packaging?

Q24. What can be said about the speaker when she says this: "Okay, if everyone is back from their break, let's start. We've got a long way to go and not much time left."

Answer Key

Q20. ⓒ Q21. ⓓ Q22. ⓐ Q23. ⓒ
Q24. ⓑ

Conversation

Listening Script

Listen to a conversation between a student and a teaching assistant.

M: Hi, Sally. What's up?

W: Hi, James. Um, actually, I came to talk to you about my group project.

M: Okay, you're in group B, right?

W: Yeah, I am. But, I'd like to change group if it's possible.

M: Really? Any problems?

W: Well, sort of. The people in my group don't seem very interested in working together.

M: Hmm, is that a good reason to switch group? I mean, making an effort to work together as a group is also one of the objectives of this project.

W: I understand that. *But... um, how should I say this...* you see, I don't think the other members are really committed to this project.

M: *You must have a good reason for saying that. Well, keep going.*

W: I mean, I believe that we need to set our priorities as full time students. I'd put my school work above everything.

M: And you believe the others are not doing that?

W: Well, out of 6 people, I'm the only one who has shown up for all three meetings so far.

M: Really? That's too bad.

W: That's not all. What's worse is that most of them show up unprepared. I feel like I'm the only one in this group who cares about the project.

M: Well, Sally, I can see how frustrating this is for you. But, unfortunately, it's too late to put you in a different group.

W: I was afraid you'd say that.

M: Tell you what, why don't I meet with your group a couple of times? Maybe it'll give them a push.

W: Really? That might really help actually. But, you would actually make time for us?

M: Sure, I don't mind. So, you can text me when you guys set up the next meeting?

W: I'll do that. Thank you so much.

Now, get ready to answer the questions.

Q25. What is the woman's problem?

Q26. What can be said about the woman when she says this:
"But... um, how should I say this..."

Q27. What is the man's attitude toward the woman?

Q28. What does the man imply when he says this:
"You must have a good reason for saying that. Well, keep going."

Answer Key

Q25. Ⓓ Q26. Ⓐ Q27. Ⓒ Q28. Ⓒ

Winning TOEFL

Yuri Yi

Listening Step 3

Step 1
Step 2
Step 3

Wit & Wisdom is the professional language publishing company of the **PAGODA** Education Group.

Copyright ⓒ 2010 by Yuri Yi

All rights reserved. No part of this publication may be reproduced, stored
in a retrieval system, or transmitted, in any form, or by any means, electronic,
mechanical, photocopying, recording or otherwise, without the prior written
permission of the copyright holder and the publisher.

Published by PAGODA Books
PAGODA Books is the professional language publishing company of the
PAGODA Education Group.
19F, PAGODA Tower, 419, Gangnam-daero,
Seocho-gu, Seoul, 06614, Rep. of KOREA
www.pagodabook.com

First published 2010
First impression 2010
Twelfth impression 2024
Printed in the Republic of Korea

ISBN 978-89-6281-062-2 (13740)

Publisher | Kyung-Sil Park
Writer | Yuri Yi

Winning TOEFL iBT

Listening Step 3

Wit&Wisdom

Wit&Wisdom is the professional language publishing company of the PAGODA Education Group.

Introduction to iBT TOEFL

iBT TOEFL (internet-based TOEFL) is designed to measure how well non-native speakers of English read, listen, speak, and write in English. The test has four sections: reading, listening, speaking, and writing. Each section of the test is worth 30 points and the highest possible score on the iBT is 120 points (30 points x 4 sections). Most questions are worth 1 point each, but some of the questions in each section are worth more than 2 points.

 → For more information, visit the ETS website (www.ets.org).

Listening Section

(1) About the listening material

In the listening section, test takers are asked to listen to 4 or 6 lectures and 2 or 3 conversations. The length of each material varies from 500 to 800 in words, or 3 to 5 minutes in listening time.

Number of Passages	Types of Material	Test Time
6	4 Lectures 2 Conversations	60 min
9	6 Lectures 3 Conversations	90 min

There are two major types of listening material covering a wide range of topics that students need to listen in academic environment:

- Lectures: a talk given by a professor or a discussion with students on an academic subject in the classroom setting
- Conversations: a student talking to a professor, teaching assistant, school staff or employee about a situation related to student life

All material is recorded in natural spoken English from North America and other English-speaking parts of the world.

(2) About the questions

After listening to each material, several questions follow to test the ability of the test takers in the following areas:

- Basic Comprehension: ability to understand the main topic and idea of the material and detail information

WINNING TOEFL LISTENING

- Pragmatic Understanding: ability to understand the function of what is said and recognize the speaker's attitude
- Connecting Information: ability to understand organization of the material, connect content and make inferences

In order to test these areas, there are six major types of questions asked in the iBT TOEFL listening section.

Question Type	Explanation	Related Unit
Basic Comprehension		
Main topic / idea	Asks about the overall topic or the central idea of the material	Unit 1
Supporting / Specific Details	Asks about specific information that are important points within the material	Unit 2
Connecting Information		
Organization	Asks about the overall structure and flow of the material	Unit 3
Content	Asks about the relationship and reasoning of specific information within the material	Unit 4
Pragmatic Understanding		
Function	Asks about the purpose or meaning of specific information or phrases	Unit 5
Stance and Attitude	Asks about the attitude or implied meanings of the speaker	Unit 6

Winning TOEFL Listening series

This is the third listening book in *Winning TOEFL* series. It has 6 units, and each unit includes 6 lectures and 3 conversations in various lengths.

This third book is designed for students who are beginners in academic listening. Therefore, the level of difficulty and the length of the listening material have been modified from the original materials seen on the actual TOEFL.

Each unit of this book deals with a specific academic topic and situation that appear frequently on the TOEFL:

	LECTURE TOPICS	CONVERSATION TOPICS
Unit 1	Natural Science	School admission and registration
Unit 2	History	Class activities
Unit 3	Applied Sciences	Student jobs
Unit 4	Minds and Behaviors	Student housings
Unit 5	Nature and Society	Student activities
Unit 6	Arts and Culture	School policies and facilities

Each unit consists of:

Introduction ➜ Practices I, II ➜ Tests 1, 2, 3 ➜ Listening Helper

Each section has the following subsections.

Introduction

(1) Key Expressions

Key Expressions are provided to help students become familiar with frequently used expressions in academic settings. Each unit carries different set of expressions that may be used with specific intentions. Students should pay attention to these expressions as signals for more important information while they are listening.

(2) Target iBT TOEFL Questions

This part is to prepare students with frequently asked question types in the iBT TOEFL listening test. Students are encouraged to listen for type of information that is more likely to appear in the questions. Each unit focuses on the following iBT TOEFL question types:

Unit 1	Main idea and Topic Questions
Unit 2	Specific Detail Questions
Unit 3	Organization Questions
Unit 4	Content Questions
Unit 5	Function Questions
Unit 6	Attitude Questions

Practice 1, 2

The main purpose of this section is to lead students to listen to short passages (185 words in average) and find answers for target questions. Additional exercises with specific tasks follow to strengthen student's skills for keyword listening and summarization.

(1) Warm Up

This part is provided as a pre-listening exercise. Students are asked to complete each sentence using words from the box below. The purpose of this exercise is to familiarize students with the content of the lectures or discussions in the practice section.

(2) Part I: Practice 1, 2, 3 - With dictation exercises

In this part, students are asked to answer one target question for each listening material. Then the following dictation exercise asks students to listen again to fill in the blanks in the script provided. This exercise is designed to help students practice listening skills on linking sounds and sound confusions.

(3) Part II: Practice 4, 5, 6 - With summary exercises

In this part, students are asked to answer 2-3 questions including target questions for each listening material. Then the following summary exercise asks students to listen again to complete the summary notes. This exercise is designed to lead students to understand the overall flow of the material and be able to extract its key information.

(4) Vocabulary

Each practice question is provided with the list of key vocabulary. This list can be studied before students listen to the material in order to enhance students' understanding. It can also be reviewed afterward in the Listening Helper section.

Tests 1, 2, 3
In this section, students are required to listen to longer material (270 words in average) and answer 4-5 questions including each unit's target questions. This section is an opportunity for students to apply their skills acquired from the unit into more intensive practice.

Listening Helper
This part is provided to help students review and strengthen their knowledge of essential vocabulary. Students are asked to listen to each statement and complete it with the correct vocabulary. Each statement and the vocabulary have been taken from the practice section.

Actual Test
At the end of all 6 units, one set of actual test is provided. In this section, there are 6 listening materials (4 academic lectures and 2 conversations) followed by 3-5 questions. Although the lengths and the difficulty of the material have been modified to meet beginner's level, students are encouraged to take this section as an actual test taking opportunity.

WINNING TOEFL LISTENING

Contents

Unit 1   Academic Lectures : Natural Science
                Conversations   010

Unit 2   Academic Lectures : History
                Conversations   028

Unit 3   Academic Lectures : Applied Sciences
                Conversations   046

Unit 4   Academic Lectures : Minds and Behaviors
                Conversations   064

Unit 5   Academic Lectures : Nature and Society
                Conversations   082

Unit 6   Academic Lectures : Arts and Culture
                Conversations   100

●● **Actual Test**   118

●● **Script & Answer Keys**

UNIT 01

Academic Lectures: Natural Science Conversations

•• Key Expressions

The speaker may use certain expressions as a signal to talk about the main topic or idea of the lecture.

- What I'd like to discuss now is...
- Let's look more closely at...
- I want to explain...
- Today, we're going to examine...

- Are you familiar with...?
- Do you know...?
- The interesting thing is...
- I'd like to begin by discussing...

•• Target iBT TOEFL Questions

Academic lectures

What is the main topic of the lecture/discussion?
What does the speaker mainly discuss?
What is the main idea of the lecture?

Conversations

What is the conversation mainly about?
What are the speakers mainly discussing?
Why does the student go to the registrar's office?

Practices

Warm Up 🔊 01_U1_WU.mp3

Use the picture and the vocabulary from the box below to fill in the blanks in each sentence. Then listen to the recording to check your answers.

1. Certain _____ specialize in particular jobs within their _____.

2. Seismic waves are the vibrations caused by _____.

3. Many scientists believe that the _____ were killed by an impact of a _____.

4. Many people wonder if animals have _____ like humans do.

5. The dinosaurs probably had certain _____ that helped their _____.

6. Climate change is making it more difficult to preserve _____ animals like _____.

| meteorite | survival | emotions | features | endangered |
| colonies | earthquakes | ants | polar bears | dinosaurs |

Part I

Practice 1

A Listen to part of a lecture given in a biology class. Pay attention to the main topic or idea and answer the question.

Q. What does the speaker mainly discuss?

Ⓐ Two different colonies of ants
Ⓑ Special skills for carrying larvae
Ⓒ The specialized ants
Ⓓ The importance of worker ants

B Listen again and fill in the blanks.

Prof(W): Scientists have noticed that ants tend to _____ in jobs within their _____. However, they also noticed that having the specialty doesn't necessarily make them _____ _____. A group of biologists studied rock ants to _____ _____ how they actually work. In one of their experiments, they forced the _____ colony of rock ants to _____ to a new artificial nest. When they moved, there were certain ants that specialized in carrying the larvae as their _____ job, but there were also others that did various jobs _____ carrying larvae. So, the biologists _____ the two groups of ants for the _____ and the _____ of their work. They found that the ants that only carried larvae were not working faster or better than other ants. So, they concluded that specialized ants weren't any more _____ than ants that do every job in the colony.

• tend to	to be inclined to
• colony	**n** a group of the same kind of animals living together
• specialize	**v** to concentrate on a particular activity or product
• specialty	**n** a special skill or characteristic
• figure out	to solve; discover; understand
• artificial	**adj** made by human beings; synthetic; non-natural
• larva	**n** the newly hatched form of an insect (pl. larvae)
• efficient	**adj** effective; productive

Practice 2  03_U1_P2.mp3

A Listen to part of a lecture in a science class. Pay attention to the main topic or idea and answer the question.

Q. What is the main topic of the lecture?

Ⓐ An important geologic discovery
Ⓑ Calculating the speed of seismic waves
Ⓒ The most accurate picture of the Earth's interior
Ⓓ Two different types of earthquakes

B Listen again and fill in the blanks.

Prof(M): In the early 20th century, scientists discovered seismic waves which are the vibrations _____ earthquakes. They found that seismic waves traveled thousands of miles through the _____ of the Earth. This discovery was _____ to geologists because it helped them study and gain a more _____ picture of the Earth's interior. Geologists concluded that these vibrations were of two types: _____, or P waves and _____, or S waves. So, P waves travel through both _____ and solids while S waves travel only through solid materials. They also found that P waves _____ _____ at a certain depth but still continued traveling _____ into the Earth's interior. On the other hand, S waves disappeared or were _____ back. Eventually, geologists were able to _____ the depth of the _____ between the solid mantle and the liquid core within the Earth's interior.

• seismic	**adj**	of or caused by an earthquake
• vibration	**n**	tremor; trembling
• compression	**n**	the process of putting pressure
• shear	**n**	the process of moving as if by cutting
• boundary	**n**	border; limit

Practice 3  04_U1_P3.mp3

A Listen to part of a conversation in a school office. Pay attention to the main situation and answer the question.

Q. What is the student's problem?

Ⓐ She can't decide on which elective to study.
Ⓑ She missed the deadline to add a course.
Ⓒ She is taking too many courses.
Ⓓ She is unable to drop her course.

B Listen again and fill in the blanks.

W: Excuse me. I need to _____ a course change. Can you help me with that?

M: Yes, but you should know that the _____ to add courses has already _____.

W: Oh, I see. But, I just need to _____ a course. I can still do that, can't I?

M: Sure, you can. May I ask why, _____?

W: Well, I thought I could _____ six courses in a semester. But, it is a little _____.

M: Six is a lot indeed. Well, dropping a course might be a _____ decision then.

W: Yeah. So, I'm dropping one of my _____.

M: Okay. Now, let me just _____ the system here. And, I'll need your student ID number.

- overwhelming   **adj** overpowering; being affected strongly
- indeed   **adv** without a doubt; certainly
- elective   **n** a subject which a student can choose to study

Part II

 05_U1_P4.mp3

A Listen to part of a lecture in a science class. Then answer the following questions.

Q1. What is the main topic of the lecture?

 Ⓐ Impact of a space rock on a Mexican peninsula

 Ⓑ A new theory on the extinction of the dinosaurs

 Ⓒ The relationship between a meteorite and volcanoes

 Ⓓ Geologic evidence of Deccan Volcanism

Q2. What does the speaker say about the massive impact by a space rock?

 Ⓐ It could have been caused by Deccan Volcanism.

 Ⓑ It probably didn't happen in the Yucatan.

 Ⓒ It might lead to a new theory about the dinosaurs.

 Ⓓ It was believed to be the cause of the extinction of the dinosaurs.

Q3. What did the research team find in studying Deccan Volcanism?

 Ⓐ Geologic samples of a massive impact by a meteorite

 Ⓑ Less and less evidence of life after each volcanic eruption

 Ⓒ Evidence of a massive existence of dinosaurs

 Ⓓ The influence of sulfur dioxide in the Yucatan peninsula

• impact	**n**	collision; crash; smash
• meteorite	**n**	a matter that has fallen from outer space to the Earth's surface
• peninsula	**n**	a piece of land that sticks out from a larger piece of land and surrounded by water
• extinction	**n**	dying out; abolition; destruction
• plateau	**n**	a large area of high and fairly flat land
• subsequent	**adj**	following; after; later

B Listen again and find the correct words from below to complete the summary.

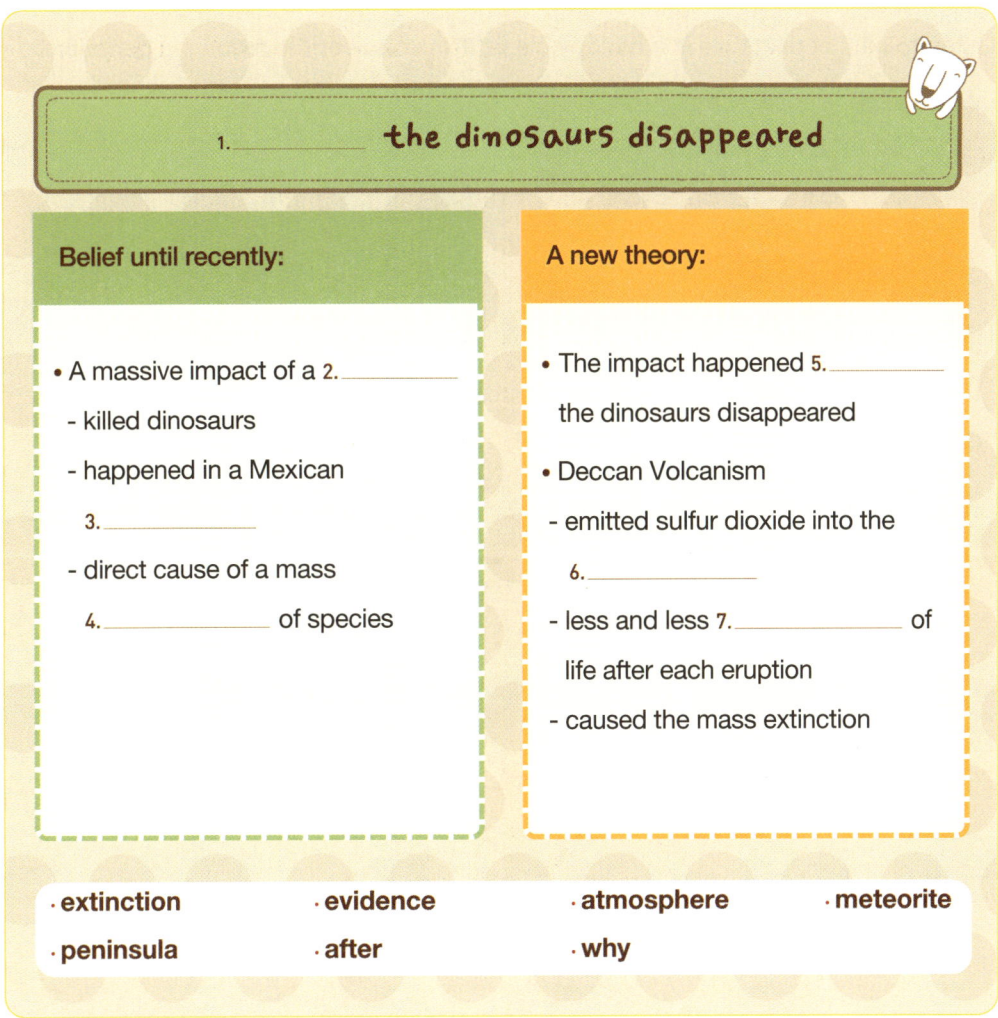

1. _____ the dinosaurs disappeared

Belief until recently:
- A massive impact of a 2. _____
  - killed dinosaurs
  - happened in a Mexican 3. _____
  - direct cause of a mass 4. _____ of species

A new theory:
- The impact happened 5. _____ the dinosaurs disappeared
- Deccan Volcanism
  - emitted sulfur dioxide into the 6. _____
  - less and less 7. _____ of life after each eruption
  - caused the mass extinction

- extinction
- evidence
- atmosphere
- meteorite
- peninsula
- after
- why

Practice 5   06_U1_P5.mp3

A Listen to part of a lecture in a biology class. Then answer the following questions.

Q1. What does the speaker mainly discuss?

- Ⓐ How to recognize animal emotions
- Ⓑ Whether animals have emotions
- Ⓒ Human influence on animal emotions
- Ⓓ Why animals have emotions

Q2. What does the speaker say about animal emotions?

- Ⓐ They are more interesting to study than human emotions.
- Ⓑ They are very different from human emotions.
- Ⓒ Captive animals have richer emotions than wild ones.
- Ⓓ They may not be as sophisticated as human emotions.

Q3. What does the speaker suggest to the students?

- Ⓐ Observe animals more carefully
- Ⓑ Show more emotions to captive animals
- Ⓒ Go to a website for more research results
- Ⓓ Try to make sense of animal emotions

• grief	n	deep emotional pain; torment
• assign	v	to place; appoint
• sophisticated	adj	refined; complicated
• conduct	v	to lead or guide; control
• captive	adj	kept under control; confined
• neuroscience	n	any of the sciences dealing with the nervous system
• get absorbed		to be wholly involved; be really into something

B Listen again and find the correct words from below to complete the summary.

Questions about animal emotions

Not as 1._____ or sophisticated as human's

A 2._____ result observing wild and 3._____ animals

On animal emotions:
- not 4._____ from human's
- richer and 5._____ expression than humans
- get completely 6._____ in the moment

Suggestion:
- animals sometimes know right from 7._____

More specific results:
- check the 8._____

- website
- research
- deeper
- specific
- absorbed
- captive
- wrong
- different

Practice 6 07_U1_P6.mp3

A Listen to part of a conversation between a student and an office staff. Then answer the following questions.

Q1. Why did the student come to the office?

   Ⓐ To hand in a formal request for his courses

   Ⓑ To get the signature of the chairperson

   Ⓒ To complain about his archaeology courses

   Ⓓ To ask about changing his major

Q2. Why does the student want to study archaeology?

   Ⓐ He is doing badly in his current courses.

   Ⓑ He feels more enthusiastic about archaeology.

   Ⓒ He likes the chairperson of the archaeology department.

   Ⓓ He wants to study two majors.

• passionate	**adj** affected by intense feeling; enthusiastic
• submit	**v** to propose or hand something in for review or decision
• chairperson	**n** the head of an organization or department

B Listen again and find the correct words from below to complete the summary.

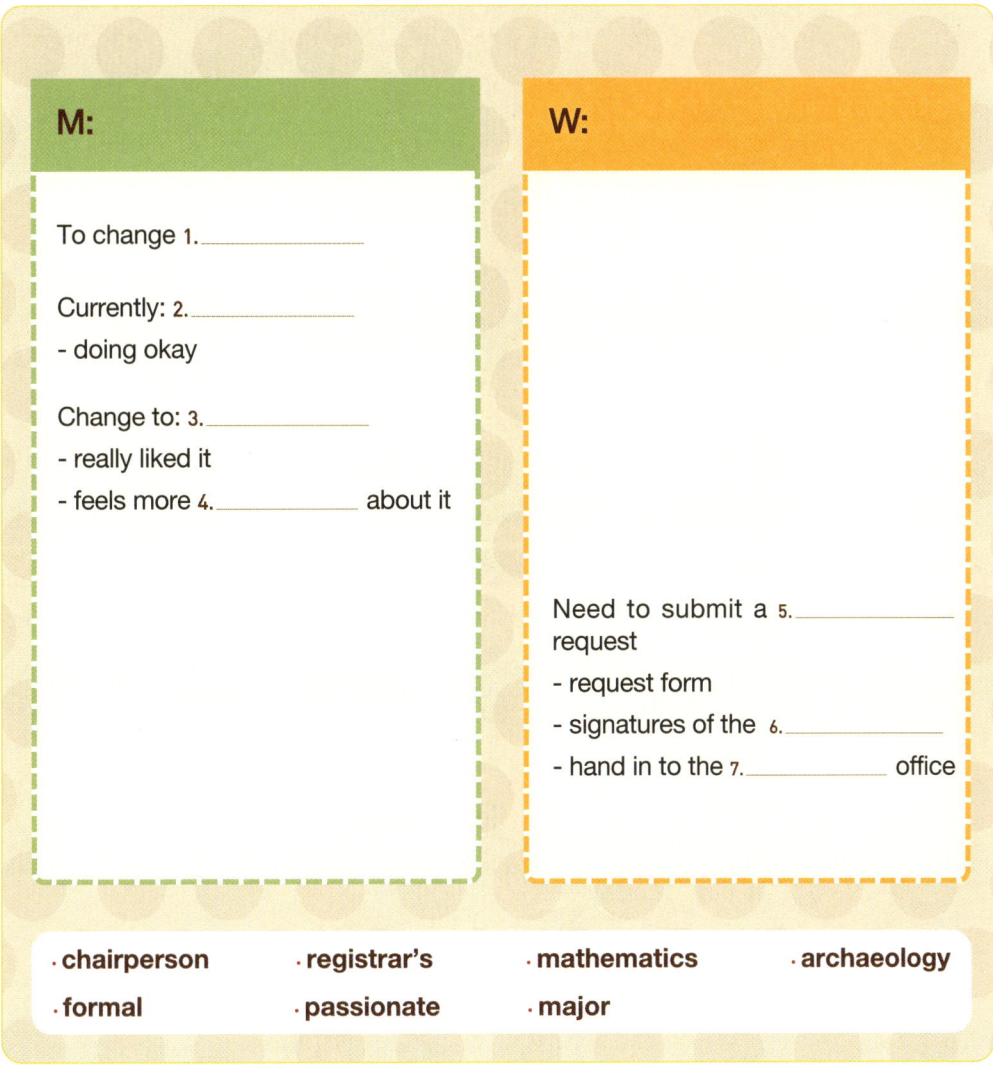

M:

To change 1._____

Currently: 2._____
- doing okay

Change to: 3._____
- really liked it
- feels more 4._____ about it

W:

Need to submit a 5._____ request
- request form
- signatures of the 6._____
- hand in to the 7._____ office

· chairperson   · registrar's   · mathematics   · archaeology
· formal   · passionate   · major

Test 1 08_U1_T1.mp3

Q1. What is the main topic of the lecture?

    Ⓐ The extinction of large species

    Ⓑ The rise of the dinosaurs

    Ⓒ The competition of the dinosaurs

    Ⓓ The diversity of ancient animals

Q2. According to the lecture, what is true about the crurotarsans?

Click on 2 answers.

    Ⓐ They were more advanced than the dinosaurs.

    Ⓑ They evolved from the dinosaurs.

    Ⓒ They went extinct during the late Triassic period.

    Ⓓ They became prevalent because of their large size.

Q3. What do many scientists think about the dinosaurs?

    Ⓐ They were probably more ancient than the crurotarsans.

    Ⓑ They didn't have any advanced features.

    Ⓒ They happened to be lucky enough to survive.

    Ⓓ They lost their competition against the crurotarsans.

Q4. According to the lecture, what happened about 200 million years ago?

　Ⓐ The dinosaurs began to grow very big.

　Ⓑ Large species became more prevalent on earth.

　Ⓒ Many species became extinct.

　Ⓓ The crurotarsans won the competition against the dinosaurs.

Q5. What does the speaker say about evolution?

　Ⓐ It can be well predicted.

　Ⓑ It depends on the period in which the species live.

　Ⓒ The size of the animals plays a big part of it.

　Ⓓ It can be a result of lucky coincidences.

- prevalent   **adj** commonly existing; prevailing
- superior   **adj** of great value; of higher nature
- Triassic period   the geologic time of the first period of Mesozoic Era, before the Jurassic Period
- adapt   **v** to become suitable to fit a specific situation
- coincidence   **n** accident; something happening by chance or luck

Test 2

Q1. What does the speaker mainly discuss?

 Ⓐ How shifts in animal habitats affect our climate

 Ⓑ The impact of temperature change on animals

 Ⓒ Butterflies as endangered species

 Ⓓ Why certain animals move to cooler areas

Q2. What is the main point of the talk?

 Ⓐ It is necessary for animals to change their habitats.

 Ⓑ Animals can survive better in cooler regions.

 Ⓒ The increase in temperature may bring critical changes.

 Ⓓ Shifts in animal habitats should be prevented.

Q3. According to the talk, how much has global temperature increased?

 Ⓐ About 1 degree Fahrenheit

 Ⓑ Exactly 2 degrees Fahrenheit

 Ⓒ 4 to 11 degrees Fahrenheit

 Ⓓ More than 6 degrees Fahrenheit

Q4. Why does the speaker mention butterflies?

    Ⓐ To show how they have become endangered species

    Ⓑ To explain a reason for the temperature change

    Ⓒ To describe how they adapt to cooler climate

    Ⓓ To give an example of changes in the animal system

Q5. What is happening to many animal species?

Click on 2 answers.

    Ⓐ They are not moving around any more.

    Ⓑ Their body temperature is getting cooler.

    Ⓒ They are changing where they live.

    Ⓓ They change their timing in doing things.

• habitat	**n**	the area or environment in which animals or plants live
• impact	**n**	influence; effect
• emerge	**v**	to rise; become clear
• endangered	**adj**	faced with the danger of extinction
• makeup	**n**	composition; arrangement
• intergovernmental	**adj**	occurring between two or more governments
• panel	**n**	a group of people who plan or discuss an issue

Test 3 🔊 10_U1_T3.mp3

Q1. What is the student's problem?

ⓐ She is unsure about when to visit the professor.

ⓑ The course she wants to register for is already full.

ⓒ She doesn't know which history course to take.

ⓓ She can't find her history classroom.

Q2. What does the professor say about history 201?

ⓐ It might be too difficult for the student to study.

ⓑ He didn't think it would be a popular course.

ⓒ It needs to be held in a small classroom.

ⓓ It deals with a lot of new material on the history of war.

Q3. What does the student mean when she says this:

ⓐ Many students are studying to surprise the professor.

ⓑ Many students also couldn't register for the course.

ⓒ The professor should meet more students.

ⓓ There are many things the professor doesn't know.

Q4. What does the professor say he will do?

ⓐ Talk to the students

ⓑ Look into the fire regulation

ⓒ Request a bigger classroom

ⓓ Not try anything

- spare   **v** to give; grant
- be in the same boat   **idiom** to be in the same situation
- frustration   **n** disappointment; dissatisfaction
- fire regulation   rules or law related to preventing and controlling fire
- petition   **n** a formal request to an authority; appeal

Listening Helper 🔊 11_U1_LH.mp3

A. Listen to each sentence and fill in the blank with the correct word(s) you hear. 🎧

1. Specialized ants weren't any more _____ than non-specialized ants.
2. P waves and S waves are two different types of _____ waves.
3. Humans sometimes try to _____ their own emotions to animals.
4. A biologist _____ an interesting research on animal emotions.
5. James realizes that he feels more _____ about history than physics.
6. Many cases of evolution may have been just lucky _____.
7. The timing for caterpillars to _____ is changing due to climate change.
8. The professor only had a few minutes to _____ for the student.
9. Many people go through _____ when they try to register for courses.
10. Over one hundred students signed a _____ to reopen the theatre on campus.

**B. First, listen to each sentence to complete the blank with the correct word(s).
Then choose the word that has the same meaning as the word from the recording.** 🎧

1. The biologists studied rock ants to _____ how they work.
   Ⓐ shape   Ⓑ understand   Ⓒ calculate

2. The rock ants were moved to a new _____ nest during the experiment.
   Ⓐ synthetic   Ⓑ artistic   Ⓒ official

3. Animals _____ completely _____ in the moment.
   Ⓐ get dried out   Ⓑ lose interest   Ⓒ get involved

4. The students need to _____ a formal request if they want to change their majors.
   Ⓐ decide   Ⓑ hand in   Ⓒ consider

5. The dinosaurs were not really _____ to other species in terms of competition.
   Ⓐ advanced   Ⓑ tolerant   Ⓒ cruel

6. We're beginning to see more _____ of the increase in global temperature.
   Ⓐ crash   Ⓑ cause   Ⓒ effect

7. There was less and less evidence of life after each _____ volcanic eruption.
   Ⓐ following   Ⓑ underground   Ⓒ related

8. Luck may be the reason why the dinosaurs became so _____.
   Ⓐ dominant   Ⓑ early   Ⓒ relevant

9. Dropping an _____ may be a wise decision.
   Ⓐ vote   Ⓑ optional course   Ⓒ election campaign

10. The student thinks his courses are a little _____.
    Ⓐ overpowering   Ⓑ ordinary   Ⓒ unusual

Natural Science •• 27

UNIT 02

Academic Lectures: History
Conversations

•• Key Expressions

The speaker may use certain expressions or words as a signal to mention important details in the lecture.

• You should remember that…	• especially
• This is actually interesting because…	• absolutely
• It's important to keep in mind…	• consider
• One thing I want to mention here is that…	• make sure
• The best way is to…	• necessary
• It is true that…	• fact

•• Target iBT TOEFL Questions

Academic lectures

What does the speaker say about…?
Which of the following is true about…?
According to the lecture, what is…?

Conversations

What is the conversation mainly about…?
What does the woman suggest to the student?

Practices

Warm Up

Use the picture and the vocabulary from the box below to fill in the blanks in each sentence. Then listen to the recording to check your answers.

1. The Silk Road was a long _____ that included _____.

2. Early generations of _____ were forced to work as _____.

3. Some _____ cultures became more important through trades and _____ strategy.

4. People with different _____ wore different clothes in the _____.

5. The _____ from each state came together to write the _____ in 1787.

6. An _____ is a good way to find out people's personal experiences during _____ events.

| black Americans | representatives | passage | past | status |
| military | deserts | small | slaves | historical | Constitution | interview |

Part I

Practice 1

A Listen to part of a lecture in a history class. Pay attention to specific details and answer the question.

Q. Which of the following is true about the Silk Road?

Click on 2 answers.

Ⓐ It was developed by a Chinese emperor.
Ⓑ It was mainly used by merchants for trading silk.
Ⓒ Merchants from the West brought silk to China.
Ⓓ It was first discovered during the Han Dynasty.

B Listen again and fill in the blanks.

Prof(W): The Silk Road first began in China during the Han Dynasty around 130 B.C.E. The _____ named Wudi learned that there was a great civilization to the _____ of his empire. Until then, Chinese people didn't know about the _____ of other civilizations besides their _____. Now, being a wise and enlightened _____, Wudi saw this new finding as the potential for trade between the two _____. In order to make trade possible, Wudi began to develop a passage that led all the way to the _____ _____ western civilization. This passage got its name 'silk road' because it was used by _____ who mainly brought silk from China to the West. Then _____ _____ to China, they brought glasses, linen and gold from the West. The Silk Road _____ about 5,000 miles of land and water including trails, bridges and deserts.

• civilization	**n**	an advanced state of cultural development in human society
• enlightened	**adj**	informed; open-minded; knowledgeable
• merchant	**n**	tradesman; dealer; retailer
• stretch across		to extend; spread

Practice 2 🔊 14_U2_P2.mp3

A Listen to part of a lecture about slavery in North America. Pay attention to specific details and answer the question.

Q. The speaker mentioned the history of slavery in North America. Check if the following group of people was mentioned as slaves or not. Put a check mark in the correct box.

	Mentioned	Not mentioned
Ⓐ War criminals from the Civil War		
Ⓑ The earliest generations of black Americans		
Ⓒ North American natives		
Ⓓ Indentured workers from Europe		
Ⓔ Criminals from Africa		

B Listen again and fill in the blanks.

> **Prof(M):** _____ popular belief, the earliest generations of black Americans were not the _____ group of slaves in North America. When the Europeans first came to the new _____ in the 16th century, they tried to _____ the native people. But, they were unsuccessful because most of the native people died of _____ when they were _____. Then the British government _____ thousands of people to come to North America. These people were called indentured servants which was a kind of _____ slavery. It was actually a way for the government to _____ _____ the less desirable members of the society like _____. Then the Europeans forced millions of African people to North America to work as slaves. In the early 1800s, there were _____ _____ Africans coming as slaves. However, the Africans who were already in North America _____ their enslaved lives _____ the Civil War.

- enslave — **v** to make into a slave
- indentured — **adj** forced to work for a period of time by some authority
- get rid of — to waste; throw away; be free from
- criminal — **n** a person who is convicted of a crime; lawbreaker

Practice 3 🔊 15_U2_P3.mp3

A Listen to part of a conversation between a student and a teacher. Pay attention to specific details and answer the question.

Q. What problem does the student have?

Ⓐ She is disappointed with her mark.
Ⓑ She made a mistake on her test.
Ⓒ Her test score was miscalculated.
Ⓓ She can't get help from her TA.

B Listen again and fill in the blanks.

> **W:** Hi, Professor. I think there is an _____ in my test score.
>
> **M:** Oh? What could that be?
>
> **W:** You gave me 80, but when I _____ _____ the marks from each question, I get a total of 82.
>
> **M:** Hmm..., you are right. I guess my TA George made a mistake with the _____.
>
> **W:** Actually, I went to see George _____ at the TA's office. But he was not there.
>
> **M:** Well, _____ it with me and I'll _____ _____ fix your mark. I'm sorry that this happened.
>
> **W:** No, no. _____ _____ it gets fixed, that's no problem.
>
> **M:** Well, you can _____ _____ me. I'll make sure of that.

- sum up   to add together
- count on   to depend on; rely on

Part II

Practice 4  16_U2_P4.mp3

A Listen to part of a lecture in a history class. Then answer the following questions.

Q1. What does the speaker mainly discuss?

  Ⓐ Why were the Aramaeans good at military conquests
  Ⓑ How a small civilization became influential
  Ⓒ The importance of language in early history
  Ⓓ The rise of dominant and wealthy civilizations

Q2. According to the speaker, why was it important for Aramaeans to control the trade routes?
Click on 2 answers.

  Ⓐ It was greatly profitable.
  Ⓑ It strengthened their military power.
  Ⓒ People in the region learned Aramaic.
  Ⓓ It enabled them to control other powerful neighbors.

Q3. What does the speaker say about Egypt and Mesopotamia?

  Ⓐ They lost their war against the Aramaeans.
  Ⓑ They eventually conquered the Aramaeans.
  Ⓒ They were the most powerful and wealthy nations.
  Ⓓ They used Aramaic as their written language.

• dominant	**adj**	main; superior; primary
• brutality	**n**	cruel and violent treatment; cruelty; inhumanity
• conquest	**n**	victory; takeover; invasion
• profitable	**adj**	money-making; beneficial; worthwhile

B Listen again and find the correct words from below to complete the summary.

Early Civlization

Important early cultures
- 1. _____ around the same period

Smaller ones
- under the influence of 2. _____ neighbors
- some grew to become important

e.g. Aramaean civilization
- known for brutality and 3. _____ conquests
- gained 4. _____ over the 5. _____ routes between Egypt and Mesopotamia
    1) profitable
    2) people 6. _____ Aramaic ➜ helped them become more
       7. _____

- dominant
- influential
- emerged
- learned
- control
- military
- trade

Practice 5

A Listen to part of a lecture in a history class. Then answer the following questions.

Q1. What is the main topic of the lecture?

Ⓐ Common fabric used for the medieval clothing
Ⓑ Paintings of Medieval Europe
Ⓒ Medieval European clothing
Ⓓ Different status of people in Medieval Europe

Q2. Why did the speaker bring the slides of the medieval paintings?

Ⓐ To show different types of social status
Ⓑ To explain why people wore tunics
Ⓒ To describe people's clothing
Ⓓ To distinguish their painters

Q3. According to the lecture, how did the noblewomen dress?

Ⓐ They generally dressed in black and white.
Ⓑ Their tunics were longer than ordinary women.
Ⓒ They wore fancy tall hats.
Ⓓ They wore loose pants.

• tunic	**n**	a sleeveless garment to be worn over other clothing
• baggy	**adj**	loose; oversize
• distinguish	**v**	to differentiate; discriminate; tell apart
• noblemen	**n**	members of the nobility in earlier times
• linen	**n**	a kind of cloth made from a plant called flax
• woolen	**adj**	made from wool or a mixture of wool
	n	clothes made of wool
• woven	**adj**	(past participle of weave) knitted; braided
• monk	**n**	a member of a male religious community that is separated from the outside world
• nun	**n**	a member of a female religious community

B Listen again and find the correct words from below to complete the summary.

Medieval European clothing

Learn from 1._____ and sculptures

Mostly wore 2._____ tunics made of linen or wool

Became more complicated and a way to 3._____ people

Men:
- mostly: tunics to their 4._____
- old men, monks, kings & noble men for parties: 5._____ tunics
- horse riders in cooler climate: wool pants
- noblemen: 6._____ tights, no pants

Women:
- mostly: two layers of tunics, socks or tights on 7._____, no pants
- noblewomen: fancy tall hats, 8._____ tunics
- nuns: black or white tunics

| · colorful | · loose | · long | · paintings |
| · knees | · legs | · woven | · distinguish |

Practice 6

A Listen to a conversation between two people. Then answer the following questions.

Q1. What is the conversation mainly about?
- Ⓐ Getting a language tutor
- Ⓑ Going to Germany to study
- Ⓒ Helping a foreign student
- Ⓓ Studying for a speech test

Q2. What does the man hope to do with the woman's cousin?
- Ⓐ Practice speaking German
- Ⓑ Improve his tutoring skills
- Ⓒ Study for a math test
- Ⓓ Meet more native German speakers

Q3. How can the man help her cousin?
- Ⓐ Teach German grammar
- Ⓑ Tutor mathematics
- Ⓒ Help out with moving
- Ⓓ Help him perfect his speech

• freeze	**v**	to become hardened into ice; hold up; stop
• work out		to solve; happen; turn out
• around the corner		nearby

B Listen again and find the correct words from below to complete the summary.

W:

3. _____ with a native German

A cousin from Germany
 - looking for a 4. _____ tutor

May work out perfect

The cousin lives around the 6. _____

Go see him right away

M:

Worried about German

1. _____ the speech test

Enjoy 2. _____

Difficult to speak

5. _____ math for 2 years

· tutored   · failed   · practice   · math   · grammar   · corner

Test 1

Q1. What does the speaker mainly discuss?
- Ⓐ Two groups of the Constitution writers
- Ⓑ Motivations behind the revolutionary war
- Ⓒ Two different views on the writing of the Constitution
- Ⓓ The most ideal and economic governing system

Q2. Who were the writers of the United States Constitution?
- Ⓐ The historians with the idealist view
- Ⓑ The representatives from each state
- Ⓒ The historians with the economic view
- Ⓓ The private business owners

Q3. According to the historians with the economic view, why did the Constitution writers encourage the government to pay off the war debt?
- Ⓐ To get their own money back
- Ⓑ To have a financially independent government
- Ⓒ To overcome the economic depressions
- Ⓓ To completely finish off the war

Q4. The speaker mentions the following statements as to what the Constitution writers wanted. Indicate whether they are part of the idealist or the economic view. Put a check mark in the correct box.

	Idealist view	Economic view
Ⓐ Liberty and democracy		
Ⓑ Strong central government		
Ⓒ Protection of private property and business		
Ⓓ Solving the problems of social chaos		

Q5. What does the speaker say about the different views on the motivations behind the writing of the Constitution?

　　Ⓐ Both views are completely inaccurate.
　　Ⓑ Both views can be considered.
　　Ⓒ The economic view is more acceptable.
　　Ⓓ The idealist view is more acceptable.

- constitution　　ⓝ the system of laws which formally states people's rights and duties
- motivation　　ⓝ incentive; reason; inspiration
- liberty　　ⓝ freedom; independence
- democracy　　ⓝ a system of government in which people choose their rulers by voting in elections
- debt　　ⓝ a sum of money that you owe someone
- economic depression　recession; economic decline
- be reflected on　to be shown; be indicated
- representative　　ⓝ agent; delegate
- creditor　　ⓝ a person who you owe money to

Test 2

Q1. What is the main topic of the lecture?
- Ⓐ Things to remember when interviewing people
- Ⓑ Five interviews on the Great Depression
- Ⓒ The Importance of personal history
- Ⓓ Different ways to talk about historical events

Q2. What does the speaker say about asking questions during an interview?
- Ⓐ Use accurate sentences
- Ⓑ Not to ask personal questions
- Ⓒ Ask open-ended questions
- Ⓓ Describe your story first

Q3. What does the speaker mean when he says this: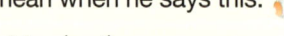
- Ⓐ He expects the student to give the answer.
- Ⓑ He wants to check if his point is understood.
- Ⓒ He asks the students to bring him something.
- Ⓓ He is unsure of what he just said.

Q4. The speaker mentions the following things about interviewing people. Indicate whether each of them is appropriate to do or not to do during an interview. Put a check mark in the correct box.

	To do	Not to do
Ⓐ Use facial expressions and body gestures		
Ⓑ Let people tell their own stories		
Ⓒ Get people to tell the truth		
Ⓓ Interfere every two minutes		
Ⓔ Write down the follow-up questions		

Q5. Why does the speaker say it is important to be sensitive during an interview?

Ⓐ Because people sometimes can't stop talking

Ⓑ Because people might get bored with the interview

Ⓒ Because people may not tell the truth

Ⓓ Because people are sharing their personal stories

- interfere — **v** to get involved although it is not wanted; intervene
- gesture — **n** signal; motion; sign
- dull look — a facial expression of boredom; plain or uninterested expression
- appropriate — **adj** suitable; fitting; well-suited
- interviewee — **n** a person who is answering the questions during an interview
- non-verbal — **adj** without words; instead of speaking
- literally — **adv** really; actually ↔ figuratively
- follow-up — something that is done to continue or add to something done previously
- cross-examination — questioning a witness already questioned by the opposing side especially during a trial

Test 3 🔊 21_U2_T3.mp3

Q1. Why does the woman come to see the man?
- Ⓐ To ask him a favor
- Ⓑ To discuss her thesis topic
- Ⓒ To print out her thesis
- Ⓓ To give him an article

Q2. What is the woman's problem?
- Ⓐ Her printer is out of order.
- Ⓑ She can't decide on her thesis topic.
- Ⓒ She is having trouble finishing her thesis.
- Ⓓ She can't get the material she needs.

Q3. What is the man going to do for the woman?
- Ⓐ Giver her access to the restricted section
- Ⓑ Print out the article she found
- Ⓒ Review the articles she wrote
- Ⓓ Find more materials for her thesis

Q4. What is the man's attitude when he says this:
- Ⓐ Reluctant
- Ⓑ Upset
- Ⓒ Willing
- Ⓓ Thankful

- drop by — to visit informally; come by
- thesis — ⓝ a long written paper based on your own ideas and research; essay
- archive — ⓝ a collection of documents and records containing historical information; chronicles
- restricted — adj limited; confined
- access — ⓝ entry; permit to go into something or somewhere
- relevant — adj significant; appropriate; related

Listening Helper 🔊 22_U2_LH.mp3

A. Listen to each sentence and fill in the blank with the correct word(s) you hear. 🎧

1. Smaller civilizations were under the influence of their _____ neighbors.
2. The Aramaean civilization was well known for their brutality and military _____.
3. Most Medieval Europeans wore tunics like big _____ shirts.
4. Using appropriate body _____ is helpful during an interview.
5. The _____ wanted the American government to pay its war debts.
6. Many students often _____ during a speech test.
7. We can always _____ Julie to get the job done.
8. Europeans tried to _____ the native people when they first came to America.
9. Sending indentured servants to America was a way to _____ criminals.
10. Students usually have access to the university _____.

B. First, listen to each sentence to complete the blank with the correct word(s).
Then choose the word that has the same meaning as the word from the recording. 🎧

1. The Silk Road _____ about 5,000 miles.
   Ⓐ grew   Ⓑ changed   Ⓒ extended

2. The writers from each state had a different _____ for writing the Constitution.
   Ⓐ reasons   Ⓑ ambitions   Ⓒ talents

3. An interviewer shouldn't _____ too often when people are telling their stories.
   Ⓐ interact   Ⓑ intervene   Ⓒ encourage

4. Emperor Wudi of the Han Dynasty was an _____ ruler.
   Ⓐ skilled   Ⓑ capable   Ⓒ open-minded

5. Clothing was a way to _____ people's status and professions.
   Ⓐ differentiate   Ⓑ upgrade   Ⓒ hide

6. The TA didn't _____ the student's marks correctly.
   Ⓐ add   Ⓑ evaluate   Ⓒ record

7. Sometimes you _____ cannot stop people from talking for over an hour.
   Ⓐ intellectually   Ⓑ actually   Ⓒ figuratively

8. The writers' need to control the social chaos was _____ the Constitution.
   Ⓐ shown in   Ⓑ contrary to   Ⓒ influenced by

9. The new library is _____.
   Ⓐ very small   Ⓑ round in shape   Ⓒ nearby

10. The professor asked the student to _____ his office.
    Ⓐ visit   Ⓑ deliver to   Ⓒ check

UNIT 03

Academic Lectures: Applied Sciences
Conversations

•• Key Expressions

The speaker may use certain expressions as a signal for the organization of certain information in the lecture.

- One example of this is…
- Let me give you some examples…
- Similarly…
- On the other hand…
- As I said before…

- The reason I mention this is…
- To prove this, the researchers…
- This shows how…
- Therefore, …
- So, as a conclusion…

•• Target iBT TOEFL Questions

Academic lectures

Why does the speaker mention…?
Why does the speaker say that…?
What does the speaker intend to show by mentioning…?
Why does the speaker say that…?

Conversations

Why does the student tell the staff about…?

Practices

Warm Up 🔊 23_U3_WU.mp3

Use the picture and the vocabulary from the box below to fill in the blanks in each sentence. Then listen to the recording to check your answers.

1. _____ are trying to track large space objects that might _____ into our planet.

2. A good amount of _____ is also important for the functioning of our _____.

3. Astronauts on space _____ need to make sure they don't run out of _____.

4. Most people carry their _____ everyday and _____.

5. Most astronauts eat frozen or _____ dried food packed in plastic wrapping.

6. It is more difficult to _____ certain items than to use newly produced ones.

oxygen	sleep	missions	cell phones	crash
vacuum	recycle	everywhere	astronomers	brain

48 •• Winning TOEFL Listening Step 3

Part I

Practice 1  24_U3_P1.mp3

A Listen to part of a talk given in an earth science class. Pay attention to how the talk is organized and answer the question.

Q. Why does the speaker mention people's attempts to blow up an asteroid?

   Ⓐ As the most critical step to prevent an impact
   Ⓑ As a less practical way to deal with a killer asteroid
   Ⓒ To explain why asteroids can be so dangerous
   Ⓓ To stress why a systematic scan of the sky is important

B Listen again and fill in the blanks.

> **Prof(W):** Nowadays, we hear more and more about the _____ of asteroid and comet strikes on Earth. Astronomers and space scientists are trying to track _____ hazardous asteroids that could cause a _____ impact on our planet. We've seen some science fiction movies or fiction illustrating people's _____ to blow the asteroid into small pieces. However, according to the experts in _____ life, such attempts would be far too expensive and _____. They say that if a killer asteroid were _____, changing its course would be the most critical step to take to prevent it from _____ the Earth. In any case, it is extremely important to _____ the existing objects in space continuously and accurately. However, many experts say that there are not enough _____ provided to conduct even a _____ scan of the sky.

• threat	**n** warning; hazard; risk
• asteroid	**n** one of the numerous small planets that move around the sun between Mars and Jupiter
• comet	**n** a bright object with a long tail that travels around the sun
• hazardous	**adj** dangerous; unsafe
• disastrous	**adj** terrible; devastating; tragic
• detect	**v** to notice; identify; recognize

Applied Sciences •• 49

Practice 2

Ⓐ Listen to part of a lecture in a health science class. Pay attention to how the speaker organizes the lecture and answer the question.

Q. How does the speaker begin the lecture?

  Ⓐ By asking a general knowledge question
  Ⓑ By introducing a surprising piece of information
  Ⓒ By doubting the belief of many sleep experts
  Ⓓ By describing evidence behind a common belief

Ⓑ Listen again and fill in the blanks.

Prof(M): There's no _____ that we need a good amount of sleep to be able to _____ properly. But, why? Why do we feel _____ when we wake up from our sleep? Sleep experts mostly _____ that sleep is important for the functioning of our brain, especially our _____. However, they disagree why and how it helps our memory. One group of experts believes that we need sleep to refresh our synapses, which _____ brain cells. According to them, we need to _____ synapses through our sleep. Otherwise, synapses become too strong and get _____ in their ability to learn and remember. So, by going to sleep, your brain will be refreshed and ready to _____ again. However, the other group of experts thinks quite the _____. They believe we need sleep to _____ and strengthen synapses which have been used while we were learning during _____ hours.

• function	n	assigned duty or activity; purpose
• refresh	v	to revive; freshen; revitalize
• synapse	n	one of the points in the nervous system at which a signal passes from one nerve cell to another
• downscale	v	to reduce in scale
• overload	v	to burden; weigh down; strain
• contrary	adj	opposed; opposite; contradictory

Practice 3   26_U3_P3.mp3

A **Listen to part of a conversation between two people. Then answer the following question.**

Q. Why did the woman ask the man to see her?

Ⓐ To see how his research is going
Ⓑ To offer him a part-time job
Ⓒ To ask him to look for a job
Ⓓ To evaluate his lab performance

B **Listen again and fill in the blanks.**

W: James, thank you for coming on such short _____.

M: No problem, Ms. Harris. I was just downstairs when you called me.

W: Oh, okay then. Now, let me just get to the _____. Are you working these days?

M: I _____ _____ _____. But, it's hard to find a part-time job these days.

W: Then, how would you like to work in my research lab... um... say ten hours a week?

M: Really? That would be great! Um, but... what would I be _____?

W: Well, just basic _____ of the lab. Nothing you can't _____ I suppose.

M: Sure. I'm _____ that you've even considered me for this job.

W: Well, the _____ is mine.

- notice   **n** announcement; communication; notification
- maintenance   **n** care; keeping; preservation; repair
- be flattered   pleased about something that makes you feel important or special

Part II

Practice 4  27_U3_P4.mp3

A Listen to a talk given in a medical engineering class. Then answer the following questions.

Q1. What is the main topic of the lecture?

Ⓐ A medical institute for astronauts

Ⓑ A new sensory device for humans

Ⓒ The importance of metabolic rate

Ⓓ A device from a spy movie

Q2. Why do astronauts need to know their metabolic rate?

Ⓐ To protect their skin

Ⓑ To get proper medical treatment

Ⓒ To plan their activities

Ⓓ To consume more oxygen

Q3. How does the speaker organize the lecture?

Ⓐ By mentioning two different uses of a device

Ⓑ By listing several interesting sensory devices

Ⓒ By describing the activities of astronauts

Ⓓ By showing how to use different skin devices

• invasive	**adj** intrusive; interfering; unwanted
• infrared light	a type of radiation that is similar to light but has a longer wavelength
• penetrate	**v** to pierce; go through; enter
• blood vessel	a narrow tube through which your blood flows
• metabolic	**adj** related to the way the chemical processes in your body cause food to be used in an efficient way such as making new cells or providing energy
• consumption	**n** using up; exhausting something through use

52 •• Winning TOEFL Listening Step 3

B Listen again and find the correct words from below to complete the summary.

A recently developed sensory 1._____

- Wearable, non-invasive
- Put on the surface of human 2._____
- Analyze the information in the person's 3._____

For astronauts:
To measure
 - the 4._____ rates
 - level of the 5._____ consumption
Why
 - to plan activities
 - not to 6._____ of oxygen

For hospital patients:
 - make sure of appropriate
   7._____
 - can 8._____ life threatening
   situation

- avoid
- skin
- run out
- oxygen
- device
- metabolic
- blood
- treatment

Practice 5

A Listen to part of a talk in an engineering class. Then answer the following questions.

Q1. What does the speaker mainly discuss?

    Ⓐ Pollution created by cell phones

    Ⓑ Using cell phones as mobile sensors

    Ⓒ How cell phones changed urban lifestyle

    Ⓓ Why it is important to carry cell phones

Q2. Why does the speaker mention computers?

    Ⓐ To compare and connect its functions with cell phones

    Ⓑ To show how he uploads his cell phone information

    Ⓒ To describe his preference over cell phones

    Ⓓ To explain an alternative to using cell phones

Q3. The speaker describes examples of the information that cell phones can collect about you. Check if each of the following is mentioned or not. Put a check mark in the correct box.

	Mentioned	Not mentioned
Ⓐ The amount of the pollution you created		
Ⓑ The type of the Internet server you use		
Ⓒ The daily amount of the exposure to pollution		
Ⓓ The size of your computer		

- context   **n** circumstance; condition; situation
- exposed   **adj** revealed; uncovered; unprotected
- sustainable   **adj** keeping in existence; maintaining
- survey   **n** examination; study; inquiry

B Listen again and find the correct words from below to complete the summary.

Cell phone

Essential 1._____ item
Carried everyday, everywhere
A new 2._____ for experimental studies

Constantly 3._____ personal information

Can tell about your 4._____

e.g.
- the amount of the pollution you 5._____
- how much you're exposed to pollution

A way to measure your 6._____ in daily life
- help to make changes to live environmentally 7._____ life

Effective and accurate ways to study people in 8._____ settings

- urban
- sustainable
- choices
- personal
- collect
- create
- lifestyle
- tool

Practice 6 🔊 29_U3_P6.mp3

Ⓐ Listen to a conversation between a student and a teacher. Then answer the following questions.

Q1. Why does the man want to see the woman?

Ⓐ He is upset about her missing classes.

Ⓑ He wants to offer her a part-time job.

Ⓒ He is concerned about her performance in class.

Ⓓ He wants to know why she comes to classes late.

Q2. What does the man offer to do for the woman?

Ⓐ Answer her questions by e-mail

Ⓑ Set up office hours on Thursdays

Ⓒ Review the class notes together

Ⓓ See her after each class

• lost	**adj**	confused; disoriented; off-track
• grasp	**v**	to catch; understand; take in

B Listen again and find the correct words from below to complete the summary.

M:

The student out of 1._____ in the class

Usually the most energetic student

Come and see after the class

3._____ on Thursdays

5._____ the questions

W:

Can't 2._____ quantum mechanics

Have to run to work

4._____ all day on Thursdays

Will try to do that

- work
- e-mail
- understand
- office hours
- focus

Applied Sciences •• 57

Test 1

Q1. What does the speaker mainly discuss?
- Ⓐ Simulation of eating on Mars
- Ⓑ How to grow vegetables in space
- Ⓒ The importance of eating together
- Ⓓ Developing dried food for astronauts

Q2. How does the speaker begin her lecture?
- Ⓐ By describing what astronauts on missions mostly eat
- Ⓑ By explaining how dried food is made
- Ⓒ By stressing the importance of a good meal in space
- Ⓓ By showing a menu she developed for NASA

Q3. What did NASA's research project in the Arctic try to experiment?
- Ⓐ Cooking meals with food from Mars
- Ⓑ Living with vacuum dried food
- Ⓒ Living on an environment similar to Mars
- Ⓓ Eating with astronauts

Q4. What is the speaker's attitude toward vacuum or frozen dried food?

Ⓐ He thinks it's fascinating.

Ⓑ He likes its taste.

Ⓒ He is curious about it.

Ⓓ He wouldn't enjoy it.

Q5. What did the astronauts in the project find to be important?

Ⓐ The taste of food

Ⓑ The vegetarian meals

Ⓒ The social aspect of eating

Ⓓ The indoor garden

• vacuum dried		having liquid material removed from a mixture under reduced air pressure
• appetizing	**adj**	tasty; delicious; tempting; appealing
• simulate	**v**	to pretend; act; put on; make an imitation
• crop	**n**	a plant that is grown in large quantities for food; produce; harvest
• ingredient	**n**	things that are used to make something especially when you are cooking
• textured	**adj**	having the surface made to have certain characteristics
• sprout	**n**	a young plant growth such as a bud or a shoot

Applied Sciences

Test 2

Q1. What is the main topic of the discussion?
- Ⓐ Effective ways to recycle
- Ⓑ Recyclable materials
- Ⓒ Process of recycling
- Ⓓ Use of recycled items

Q2. How does the professor begin the discussion?
- Ⓐ By letting the students ask questions
- Ⓑ By asking the students questions
- Ⓒ By introducing a new topic
- Ⓓ By reviewing the previous topic

Q3. Why does the professor say that computers are difficult to recycle?
- Ⓐ They are made through chemical processes.
- Ⓑ They don't have recyclable materials.
- Ⓒ They are hard to take apart for recycling.
- Ⓓ It is quite cheap to make new ones.

Q4. Which of the following is mentioned as easily recyclable?

Ⓐ Car tires

Ⓑ Food cans

Ⓒ Papers

Ⓓ Rubber

Q5. According to the discussion, what should be considered with regards to recycling?

Click on 2 answers.

Ⓐ The cost of recycling

Ⓑ The environmental benefits

Ⓒ People's preference

Ⓓ The duration of time involved

• manufacturing	**adj** being produced in a factory
• dismiss	**v** to disregard; reject; ignore
• logging	**n** the activity of cutting down trees

Applied Sciences •• **61**

Test 3

Q1. Why does the woman come to see the man?
- Ⓐ To ask some questions in French
- Ⓑ To see if she can be in his course again
- Ⓒ To check if she made it into the exchange program
- Ⓓ To ask him to review her written work

Q2. What can be said about the man?
- Ⓐ He decides who gets into the exchange program.
- Ⓑ He used to be the woman's French teacher.
- Ⓒ He is certain about the woman going to France.
- Ⓓ He was also an exchange student to France.

Q3. Why does the man say this:
- Ⓐ To encourage her to try
- Ⓑ To criticize her passive attitude
- Ⓒ To express his disappointment
- Ⓓ To point out what she's been missing or overlooking

Q4. What is the woman concerned about in applying for the exchange program?
- Ⓐ Her grades in other courses
- Ⓑ Not being in Mr. Adrienne's class
- Ⓒ The length of her French essay
- Ⓓ The lack of her French skills

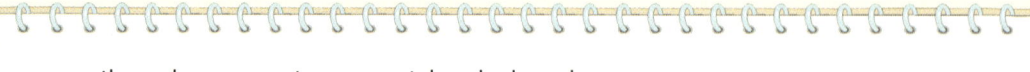

- run through   to go over; take a look; review

Listening Helper 🔊 33 _U3_LH.mp3

A. Listen to each sentence and fill in the blank with the correct word(s) you hear. 🎧

1. The _____ of asteroid and comet strikes should be taken seriously.
2. If a killer asteroid is _____ , changing its course would be the best step to take.
3. We feel _____ when we wake up from our sleep.
4. Jenny was _____ to be recommended for a job by her professor.
5. The information from the blood is used to measure the level of oxygen _____ .
6. Most people are _____ to pollution throughout the day.
7. People are making changes to live environmentally _____ lives.
8. Jane was completely _____ during her physics class.
9. Astronauts on missions usually eat _____ dried food.
10. The space crew was able to have the same food _____ as they would on earth.

B. First, listen to each sentence to complete the blank with the correct word(s). Then choose the word that has the same meaning as the word from the recording. 🎧

1. We should not _____ the environmental benefits of recycling.
   Ⓐ disregard   Ⓑ lose   Ⓒ make a mistake with

2. Synapses become too strong and get _____ in their ability to learn.
   Ⓐ freed   Ⓑ weakened   Ⓒ congested

3. The opinion raised by the other group of experts was quite the _____ .
   Ⓐ complicated one   Ⓑ opposite one   Ⓒ common one

4. Not all students can _____ working and studying at the same time.
   Ⓐ get   Ⓑ categorize   Ⓒ manage

5. The light from the sensor _____ through the skin and through the fat.
   Ⓐ sharpens   Ⓑ covers   Ⓒ enters

6. The information from your cell phone can be put into _____ and arranged.
   Ⓐ perspective   Ⓑ story   Ⓒ writing

7. George could not _____ the new theory he learned today.
   Ⓐ gain   Ⓑ understand   Ⓒ accept

8. NASA tries to develop a menu for astronauts that could be more _____ .
   Ⓐ nutritious   Ⓑ significant   Ⓒ tasty

9. The professor will _____ my essay proposal this afternoon.
   Ⓐ review   Ⓑ correct   Ⓒ hand over

10. It is important for a medical device not to be _____ on the patient's daily life.
    Ⓐ forceful   Ⓑ passive   Ⓒ intrusive

Applied Sciences

UNIT 04

Academic Lectures: Minds and Behaviors
Conversations

•• Key Expressions

The speaker may use certain expressions as a signal for implied or indirect meanings in the lecture.

- Although…
- Not only… but also…
- It won't be difficult to believe…
- I can't stress enough how important this is…
- It is no surprise to find that…

•• Target iBT TOEFL Questions

Academic lectures

What does the speaker imply about…?
What can be inferred about…?
What does the speaker mean when he says…?

Conversations

What does the student mean when she says…?
What does the professor imply about…?
What can be inferred about the student from the conversation?

Practices

Warm Up 🔊 34_U4_WU.mp3

Use the picture and the vocabulary from the box below to fill in the blanks in each sentence. Then listen to the recording to check your answers.

1. _____ interaction is an important element of being _____.

2. _____ are well known for their unusual _____.

3. Chimpanzees can be _____ to _____ phone numbers.

4. Some people seek more _____ in _____ than others.

5. Children's _____ involve pointing fingers, raising their arms, or stomping their feet.

6. A lot of _____ is involved in not getting lost in a _____.

| hyenas | human | rainforest | life | gestures | remember |
| giggles | memory | adventures | social | trained | |

Part I

Practice 1 🔊 35_U4_P1.mp3

A Listen to part of a lecture in an anthropology class. Pay attention to the implied meaning and answer the question.

Q. What can be inferred about the size of human brain?

Ⓐ It grew as humans developed social intelligence.
Ⓑ It is not relevant to the evolution of humans.
Ⓒ It makes humans unique among other species.
Ⓓ It is not a critical element in social interaction.

B Listen again and fill in the blanks.

> **Prof(W):** One of the most important features that _____ humans would be social interaction. Many anthropologists say that how we _____ to interact with each other or, our social intelligence enabled humans to be _____ among other species. I would go _____ to say that it was perhaps a critical _____ in our evolution. Looking at fossil records and other archeological _____ of behavior, it seems that the size of human brain _____ about 250 percent in less than 3 million years. I believe that humans required large brains _____ work their ways in different social situations and _____. I mean, there were competition, cooperation and other types of interactions that we had to deal with other humans. So, naturally, social interaction and social intelligence became more and more important _____ human evolution. The anthropologists go so far as to say that it was social intelligence that _____ humans to evolutionary success.

- define — **v** to explain; characterize; describe
- anthropologist — **n** one who is involved in scientific studies of human culture
- archeological — **adj** of studies that involve people or societies of the past by examining the objects from that period
- cooperation — **n** collaboration; working together; support

Practice 2

A Listen to part of a lecture about animal behavior. Pay attention to the implied meaning and answer the question.

Q. What does the speaker imply about hyenas when he says this:

Ⓐ Hyenas are mysterious animals.
Ⓑ Hyenas have their own language.
Ⓒ Hyena language is still questionable.
Ⓓ Hyenas tend to surprise people.

B Listen again and fill in the blanks.

Prof(M): Hyena language can be an _____ subject to study. Some of you might wonder if hyenas even have a language. Then, I'd say that you are ____ _____ a surprise. You see, hyenas, particularly the spotted ones are _____ social animals. And, they have a wide range of _____ communication including the giggles and groans. Actually, hyenas are quite ____ _____ for their unusual giggles, but for now, let's _____ their groans. After extensive research, experts _____ that hyenas make two types of groans. One is a low-pitched and monotonous groan. It usually gives an _____ message such as telling others to stay away from the _____ it has discovered. The other type of groan _____ between high and low pitches sounding almost like music. This kind of groan is heard a lot when a mother hyena is _____ for her cubs. It probably works as a way to reassure and _____ cubs.

• intriguing	**adj**	interesting; compelling; exciting
• spotted	**adj**	with spots (on skin or surface)
• giggle	**n**	a childlike laugh with repeated short sounds
• groan	**n**	a deep, inarticulate sound of pain or displeasures
• stick to		to remain; keep; continue
• extensive	**adj**	wide; broad; large-scale; vast; widespread
• pitch	**n**	the distinctive quality of a sound
• monotonous	**adj**	being regular; repeated without changes

Practice 3  37 _U4_P3.mp3

A Listen to part of a conversation in a housing office. Pay attention to the implied meaning and answer the question.

Q. What can be inferred about the man?

Ⓐ He already brought in his luggage.
Ⓑ He lost the key to his room.
Ⓒ His luggage was too heavy to unload by himself.
Ⓓ He didn't want to bring his luggage to the front.

B Listen again and fill in the blanks.

> **M:** Hello, my name is Jackson Hunt _____ for room 312. I'm here to pick up my keys.
>
> **W:** Oh, you must be the new student. Do you have your luggage _____ you?
>
> **M:** Actually, they're in my father's car. He's waiting in the parking lot to _____ my stuff.
>
> **W:** I see. Here's the key to your room and the magnetic card for the main entrance.
>
> **M:** Is there _____ _____ I can come in through the back _____ from the parking lot?
>
> **W:** Sure, the magnetic key also works for the back door. You _____ _____ _____ drag your luggage all the way to the front door.
>
> **M:** Oh, great. I _____ _____ I would have to do that.

• sign in	to officially record your arrival at a hotel or for an event
• unload	ⓥ to empty; unpack; discharge
• drag	ⓥ to pull along with difficulty; bring by force

Part II

A Listen to part of a lecture in a psychology class. Then answer the following questions.

Q1. What does the speaker mainly discuss?

　Ⓐ Why college students have poor memory
　Ⓑ How to test chimpanzees' memory
　Ⓒ Teaching chimpanzees to learn Arabic numbers
　Ⓓ Comparing chimpanzees' memory to humans'

Q2. How does the speaker organize the lecture?

　Ⓐ By explaining his point through the result of an experiment
　Ⓑ By comparing the students' memory to a chimpanzee's
　Ⓒ By involving the students in an interesting experiment
　Ⓓ By explaining his own experience with chimpanzees

Q3. What can be inferred about the college students in the experiment?

　Ⓐ They learned their Arabic numbers at the age of five.
　Ⓑ Their memory was interrupted by the chimpanzees.
　Ⓒ They couldn't perform as well as the chimpanzees.
　Ⓓ They performed better than chimpanzees with eight numbers.

• flash	**v** to show; display; appear suddenly
• randomly	**adv** without any specific pattern or purpose
• recall	**v** to remember; bring to mind

B Listen again and find the correct words from below to complete the summary.

Chimpanzee memory test

A five-year-old chimpanzee:
- can 1._____ phone numbers

An experiment:
- compare chimpanzees' 2._____ to humans'
- trained three chimpanzees to learn numbers from 1 to 9
- computer monitor 3._____ numbers

Chimps :
- remembered the 4._____ of the numbers in correct 5._____
- had no problem with 8 numbers

College students:
- 6._____ after 5 numbers

· flashed   · struggled   · order   · location
· memory   · recall

Practice 5  39_U4_P5.mp3

A Listen to part of a lecture in a behavioral science class. Then answer the following questions.

Q1. What is the main topic of the lecture?

  Ⓐ Benefits of being an adventure seeker
  Ⓑ A scientific explanation for those who seek adventures
  Ⓒ Different types of neural fiber connections
  Ⓓ Relationship between personalities and activities

Q2. According to the lecture, what can be inferred about the people who play extreme sports?

  Ⓐ They never like to stay home and read.
  Ⓑ Parts of their brain have stronger fiber connections.
  Ⓒ Their personality is much stronger than others.
  Ⓓ They generally receive many rewards in life.

Q3. The speaker talks about a few processes involved in a neuroscientific study. Check if the following was involved in the processes. Put a check mark in the appropriate box.

	Involved	Not involved
Ⓐ Bungee jumping		
Ⓑ Questionnaires		
Ⓒ Brain imaging		
Ⓓ Trying new experiences		

• wired into	determined or put into effect by physiological or neurological mechanisms
• seeker	**n** someone who is looking for or trying to get something
• neuroscientific	**adj** of or related to neuroscience
• extreme sports	types of sports involving high levels of risk
• reward	**n** repayment; return; prize
• fill out	to write information in the spaces of a form or document
• imaging	**n** the process of forming images; visualization of internal bodily organs
• neural fiber	a thin piece of flesh connecting nerve cells

B Listen again and find the correct words from below to complete the summary.

Personality and brain structure

Looking for adventures:
- a part of your 1._____ makes you an adventure seeker

A neuroscientific study:
- seeking adventures 2._____ with the brain
- two parts in the brain connect new experiences with a sense of 3._____

1) Fill out questionnaires to determine adventure seeking 4._____

2) Brain imaging technique:
5._____ neural fiber connection

→ Adventure seekers had 6._____ fiber connections
→ Personality might be based on the 7._____ and function of brain

- structure
- personality
- brain
- reward
- stronger
- associated
- examines

Practice 6 🔊 40 _U4_P6.mp3

A Listen to part of a conversation between a student and a housing officer. Then answer the following questions.

Q1. Why does the student come to the office?
- Ⓐ To find out where her room is
- Ⓑ To see if she can move in early
- Ⓒ To check out of her summer residence
- Ⓓ To ask if she can move in next month

Q2. What can be inferred about the woman from the conversation?
- Ⓐ She would rather not go to her parents' house.
- Ⓑ She is worried about her parents' situation.
- Ⓒ She wants to move out of her parents' place.
- Ⓓ She has been looking for an apartment.

• residency	**n** staying in a particular place
• check out	to leave a hotel or clinic where you've been staying
• burden	**v** to trouble; weigh down

B Listen again and find the correct words from below to complete the summary.

M:

Moving scheduled for next month

3. _____ resident moving out early

Can make an 4. _____

Have to pay for extra two weeks

W:

1. _____ to a residence room

Want to move in early - two weeks

Need to move out early from her 2. _____

Didn't want to burden the 5. _____

· parents   · apartment   · exception   · summer   · assigned

Test 1

Q1. What does the speaker mainly discuss?

Ⓐ The effect of gesturing on children's vocabulary

Ⓑ How children learn from other children

Ⓒ Understanding children's ideas through their gestures

Ⓓ Children's gestures that have special meaning

Q2. Which of the following would affect children's vocabulary?

Click on 2 answers.

Ⓐ Parents who speak to them a lot

Ⓑ Picking up gestures from adults

Ⓒ Starting kindergarten at an early age

Ⓓ Communicating only with fingers and arms

Q3. What do the researchers suggest gesturing does for children?

Ⓐ It causes them to have a higher vocabulary.

Ⓑ It helps the development of their fingers and arms.

Ⓒ It helps them speak more with their parents.

Ⓓ It encourages their creative thinking.

Q4. What does the speaker imply when she says this: 🎧

Ⓐ It is not clearly known why children make gestures.
Ⓑ Children gesturing can be more significant.
Ⓒ She doesn't think children gesturing is very cute.
Ⓓ Children make gestures to please adults.

Q5. What is the speaker's point about children's gesturing and vocabulary acquisition?

Ⓐ They affect children after 14 months.
Ⓑ They often happen spontaneously.
Ⓒ They shouldn't be encouraged too much.
Ⓓ They are closely associated with each other.

- spontaneous — **adj** unplanned; impulsive; natural; instinctive
- linguist — **n** someone who studies the science of language
- pick up — to learn; acquire
- kindergarten — **n** an informal kind of school for very young children
- acquisition — **n** gaining possession of something
- linked — **adj** connected; associated

Q1. What is the main topic of the lecture?

- Ⓐ Animals living in large groups
- Ⓑ Elephants having good memories
- Ⓒ Social settings of elephants
- Ⓓ Brain size of animals in a rainforest

Q2. How does the speaker describe the environment of a rainforest?

Click on 2 answers.

- Ⓐ Surprising
- Ⓑ Complicated
- Ⓒ Impressive
- Ⓓ Huge

Q3. Which of the following requires elephants to have good memories?

Click on 2 answers.

- Ⓐ Living in a jungle
- Ⓑ Competing with chimpanzees
- Ⓒ Social settings
- Ⓓ Having large brains

Q4. What does the speaker imply about the large brain size of elephants?

  Ⓐ It may be the result of their complicated memory.

  Ⓑ It doesn't really affect their memory.

  Ⓒ It is natural for any land animal.

  Ⓓ It causes them to get lost in the jungle.

Q5. According to the speaker, what is impressive about the social settings of elephants?

  Ⓐ They can distinguish every member in their group.

  Ⓑ They have very complicated social relationships.

  Ⓒ They go to different places to get their food.

  Ⓓ They spread themselves over a thousand square miles.

- rainforest   **n** a thick forest of tall trees found in tropical areas; jungle
- weigh   **v** to have a weight of
- store   **v** to keep; reserve; deposit; save

Test 3

Q1. Why does the man come to the office?
- Ⓐ To complain about the custodian
- Ⓑ To have someone repair things in his room
- Ⓒ To speak to the custodian in person
- Ⓓ To get someone to open his window

Q2. Why did the man sleep with his window open last night?
- Ⓐ The radiator gave out too much heat.
- Ⓑ He couldn't close it.
- Ⓒ He forgot to close it.
- Ⓓ He didn't think it was cold.

Q3. Listen again to part of the conversation. Then answer the question.

What does the woman imply when she says this:
- Ⓐ The problem might be a serious one.
- Ⓑ It is not good to have that much noise.
- Ⓒ The man must have heard it wrong.
- Ⓓ She has never heard such a problem.

Q4. Listen again to part of the conversation. Then answer the question.

What can be inferred from this?
- Ⓐ The custodian didn't have the tools.
- Ⓑ The custodian was too busy to help him.
- Ⓒ The man has never met the custodian.
- Ⓓ The man couldn't find the custodian.

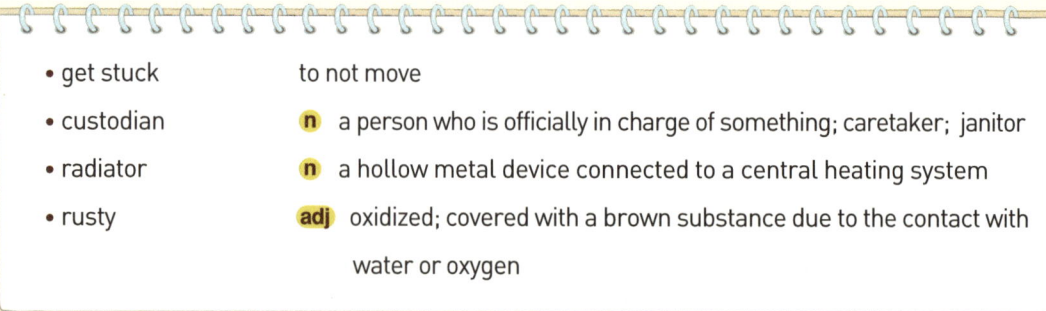

- get stuck — to not move
- custodian — **n** a person who is officially in charge of something; caretaker; janitor
- radiator — **n** a hollow metal device connected to a central heating system
- rusty — **adj** oxidized; covered with a brown substance due to the contact with water or oxygen

Listening Helper 🔊 44_U4_LH.mp3

A. Listen to each sentence and fill in the blank with the correct word(s) you hear. 🎧

1. Humans have to deal with _____ and competition with other humans.
2. The professor tried to _____ his main topic throughout the lecture.
3. A _____ hyena groan usually gives an aggressive message.
4. The number appeared _____ on a touch screen and then disappeared.
5. Chimpanzees were able to _____ the phone numbers correctly.
6. An adventure seeking personality might _____ one's brain.
7. The residents have to pay for the extra two weeks of their _____.
8. A certain type of hyena groan works as a way to _____ the cubs.
9. John had no _____ in finding the book he wanted.
10. Gesturing and vocabulary _____ of young children are closely linked with each other.

B. First, listen to each sentence to complete the blank with the correct word(s). Then choose the word that has the same meaning as the word from the recording. 🎧

1. Social interaction is one of the features that _____ humans.
   Ⓐ characterizes   Ⓑ limits   Ⓒ delivers

2. Tom is going to _____ his boxes from the car.
   Ⓐ remove   Ⓑ unleash   Ⓒ dismiss

3. David had to _____ his heavy luggage to his science lab.
   Ⓐ stretch   Ⓑ pull   Ⓒ spin

4. The subjects of the experiment had to _____ some questionnaires.
   Ⓐ build   Ⓑ answer   Ⓒ provide

5. The students are reluctant to _____ their parents.
   Ⓐ value   Ⓑ trouble   Ⓒ argue

6. Many children can _____ gestures from adults.
   Ⓐ lift   Ⓑ acquire   Ⓒ receive

7. Elephants can _____ complicated memories of their environment.
   Ⓐ put away   Ⓑ keep   Ⓒ supply

8. The revolving door _____ while I was in it.
   Ⓐ didn't move   Ⓑ closed   Ⓒ was pushed

9. The housing officer will ask the _____ to look at the window.
   Ⓐ caretaker   Ⓑ guardian   Ⓒ constructor

10. We often see children making _____ gestures.
    Ⓐ soft   Ⓑ impulsive   Ⓒ similar

Minds and Behaviors

UNIT 05

Academic Lectures: Nature and Society
Conversations

•• Target iBT TOEFL Questions

Academic lectures

What does the speaker mean when he says this?
What is the speaker's purpose when she says this?
Listen again to part of the lecture. Why does the speaker say this?

Conversations

Why does the student say this?
What does the professor mean when she says this?
Listen again to part of the conversation. Why does the man say this?

Practices

Warm Up 🔊 45_U5_WU.mp3

Use the picture and the vocabulary from the box below to fill in the blanks in each sentence. Then listen to the recording to check your answers.

1. Taming wild _____ also led people to adapt to drinking _____.

2. The supply of _____ is becoming a big problem in many parts of the world.

3. Nowadays, more people live _____ lives and remain _____.

4. The life of _____ humans changed greatly after they discovered _____.

5. More people cross their country's _____ for a better life elsewhere.

6. People often became sharecroppers when they didn't own any _____ to grow _____.

fresh water	milk	fire	animals	crops
land	borders	longer	healthier	early

Part I

Practice 1

A Listen to part of a lecture in an anthropology class. Pay attention to the meaning and purpose of special expressions and answer the question.

Q. What does the speaker mean when she says this:

Ⓐ She wants to change the topic.
Ⓑ She wants to discuss a new idea.
Ⓒ She disagrees with what has been said.
Ⓓ She is going to explain this in more detail.

B Listen again and fill in the blanks.

Prof(W): Humans have been able to _____ to changes in the environment, both genetically and uh, culturally. The fact that we have _____ fingers and binocular vision is the _____ of our genetic evolution. We also went through cultural evolution by learning how to farm, and how to write and _____ history. Furthermore, we've changed our own environment then evolved as well _____ those changes. Think about the _____ of wild animals. When some people began taming animals, they also began drinking milk. This eventually changed our body to _____ lactose from milk. Now, let's look at this from a different _____. How about the future? Well, I believe that it's our ability to _____ to the changes in the environment that may _____ us in the future. For example, _____ burning fossil fuels for energy, we could try to adapt to _____ energy sources such as solar-hydrogen energy.

• genetic	**adj**	affecting or affected by genes
• binocular	**adj**	involving both eyes at the same time
• domestication	**n**	bringing wild animals or plants under control and using them
• tame	**v**	to control; discipline; train
• lactose	**n**	a type of sugar found in milk and sometimes added to food
• alternative	**adj**	different; another; substitute

Nature and Society •• **85**

Practice 2   47_U5_P2.mp3

A Listen to part of a lecture in a human geography class. Pay attention to the purpose of special expressions and answer the question.

Q. Listen again to part of the lecture. Then answer the question.

Why does the speaker say this:

Ⓐ To stress the information he just said
Ⓑ To express his frustration
Ⓒ To show his excitement
Ⓓ To ask for the students' opinion

B Listen again and fill in the blanks.

Prof(M): There is a _____ concern about the supply of fresh water worldwide. Many of us living in _____ nations have no difficulty getting _____ drinking water. So, we _____ our access to fresh water _____ _____ and don't realize how this could be a serious problem in other parts of the world. In fact, there are more than a _____ people around the world that don't have access to fresh water, _____ _____ drinking water. Now, the number gets more _____ when we count people who don't have access to _____ sanitation services. That would be 2.5 billion people which means about 40 percent of the world's population! Think about that! In fact, the _____ sanitation service is quite critical because that could _____ _____ water-related diseases. And as you're already _____ _____, water-related diseases lead to a large number of deaths of _____ young children.

- worldwide   **adj** globally; generally; universally
- take for granted   not to appreciate or value something
- sanitation service   a service for keeping facilities or dwelling clean and healthy

Practice 3  48_U5_P3.mp3

A Listen to part of a conversation between two people. Pay attention to the purpose of special expressions and answer the question.

Q. What does the man mean when he says this:

  Ⓐ He is looking for something different.
  Ⓑ He prefers a different kind of tea.
  Ⓒ He only drinks coffee.
  Ⓓ He doesn't find it interesting.

B Listen again and fill in the blanks.

> **W:** Hey, Jude. Have you _____ who you're going to vote for the student president?
>
> **M:** Well, to tell you the truth, I don't even know who's _____ for the position.
>
> **W:** Are you serious? You should _____ more attention to what's going on.
>
> **M:** I'm just not _____ things like that. It's just not my _____ _____ _____.
>
> **W:** But, _____ the student president is quite important. It can change our campus life _____ _____ _____ who gets elected.
>
> **M:** I suppose. I guess I'm just too lazy to study the campaign _____ for the election.
>
> **W:** Come on, where's your school _____? At least read the campaign posters for each candidate.
>
> **M:** All right. You have a _____. I'll check them out.

• run for	to try to be elected
• not one's cup of tea	**idiom** not something one enjoys
• candidate	**n** contender; nominee; runner; competitor

Nature and Society •• **87**

Part II

Practice 4

A Listen to part of a lecture in a sociology class. Then answer the following questions.

Q1. What is the main topic of the lecture?

Ⓐ An article about the United Nations
Ⓑ The issues surrounding an ageing population
Ⓒ An increase in global population
Ⓓ The changes in the world's economy

Q2. According to the lecture, what is expected of older people?

Ⓐ To retire early from their work
Ⓑ To adapt to the societal changes
Ⓒ To compete with young people
Ⓓ To stay longer in the workforce

Q3. What does the speaker mean when she says this:

Ⓐ She wants to talk about the article before the discussion.
Ⓑ She wants the students to read the article first.
Ⓒ She thinks the article is more important than the discussion.
Ⓓ She believes that the article was taken from the discussion.

• fill in	to supply (someone) with information; inform (someone) about something
• resume	**v** to begin again; continue after an interruption
• relatively	**adv** comparatively; somewhat; rather
• ageing	**adj** becoming old
• societal	**adj** relating to society or the way it is organized
• adaptation	**n** conversion; adjustment; modification; naturalization
• workforce	**n** the total number of people in a country or region who are physically able to do a job and are available for work
• stagnate	**v** to stop changing or progressing

B Listen again and find the correct words from below to complete the summary.

Global population ageing

United nations' report on 1._____ population:
- by 2050, 1 out of 5 people over the age of 2._____.
- big increase in short time

Economic adaptation to an 3._____ population:

Key word: 4._____
- live longer and healthier ➔ 5._____ longer in the workforce
- not enough jobs for 6._____ people ➔ unemployment
- 7._____ of the world's economy

- workforce
- sixty
- stagnation
- young
- ageing
- global
- stay

Practice 5 🔊 50_U5_P5.mp3

A Listen to part of a lecture in an anthropology class. Then answer the following questions.

Q1. What does the speaker mainly discuss?

    Ⓐ The importance of tools in human culture

    Ⓑ The influence of fire on agriculture

    Ⓒ Two dramatic changes in human history

    Ⓓ The history of agriculture

Q2. What does the speaker mean when he says this: 🎧

    Ⓐ Only two events should be regarded as dramatic events.

    Ⓑ Many great leaps forward have been dismissed.

    Ⓒ There are two most important events among others.

    Ⓓ Two dramatic events caused many great leaps forward.

Q3. The speaker talks about the outcome of agriculture on humans. Check if the following has been mentioned as one of the outcomes or not. Put a check mark in the appropriate box.

	Mentioned	Not mentioned
Ⓐ Had enough food		
Ⓑ Invented needles for sewing clothes		
Ⓒ Became smarter and more social		
Ⓓ Settled in one place		
Ⓔ Started cave painting		

• boil down to	to reduce; summarize = come down to
• leap	ⓝ jump; sudden progress
• estimate	ⓥ to calculate roughly; evaluate; judge
• initiate	ⓥ to begin; open; set in motion

B Listen again and find the correct words from below to complete the summary.

The great leap forward in human history

The great leap forward:
- culture evolved 1._____ at first: primary to advanced 2._____
  ➜ sewing and painting
- more dramatic changes followed

The two most dramatic events:

1) 3._____ and use of fire
  ➜ dominate the environment
  ➜ develop human 4._____

2) Practice of agriculture
- the 5._____ step forward
  ➜ enough 6._____ to settle
  ➜ start civilization
  ➜ became 7._____ smart and social: different from other mammals

| · culture | · food | · discovery | · tools |
| · increasingly | · slowly | · biggest | |

Nature and Society • • **91**

Practice 6   51_U5_P6.mp3

A Listen to part of a conversation in a student council's office. Then answer the following questions.

Q1. Why does the man come to the office?

Ⓐ To seek advice on winning a half marathon
Ⓑ To get his money back
Ⓒ To get free campus souvenirs
Ⓓ To register for a campus event

Q2. What does the woman say about pre-registration?

Ⓐ The registration fee is refundable.
Ⓑ The student gets free souvenirs.
Ⓒ The student gets a discount on the fee.
Ⓓ The student gets free water at the reception.

Q3. What does the man mean when he says this:

Ⓐ It is a reasonable thing to do.
Ⓑ He never wants to do it.
Ⓒ He doesn't understand the reason for it.
Ⓓ There should be a better reason for doing it.

• reception	**n**	a place where people are greeted for an event
• keep in mind	**idiom**	to consider; remember
• refundable	**adj**	being able to get the money back
• show up		to come; attend; appear
• souvenir	**n**	something you buy or keep as a reminder of a holiday, place, or event

B Listen again and find the correct words from below to complete the summary.

W:	M:
Need 2._____ sheet	Sign up for the campus 1._____ marathon
$5 3._____ to be paid now or on Saturday	
Pre-registration: free t-shirt and water bottles	
	Likes free 4._____ ➔ pre-register
No money back for not 5._____	
	Will 6._____ show up
Will bring the shirt and the bottles	

- definitely
- half
- showing up
- sign-up
- fee
- souvenirs

Nature and Society •• 93

Test 1 🔊 52_U5_T1.mp3

Q1. What does the speaker mainly discuss?
- Ⓐ The benefits of living abroad
- Ⓑ The increasing trend of migration
- Ⓒ Why people migrate to the big country
- Ⓓ Planning policies for demographic changes

Q2. Listen again to part of the lecture. Then answer the question.
What does the speaker imply when she says this:
- Ⓐ The number will probably increase in the future.
- Ⓑ The effect of globalization will reduce the number.
- Ⓒ The trend of globalization will not change.
- Ⓓ The number will become less and less important.

Q3. According to the speaker, what motivates people to migrate to other countries?
Click on 2 answers.
- Ⓐ Better lifestyle
- Ⓑ Smaller population
- Ⓒ Job opportunities
- Ⓓ Friends and relatives

Q4. Listen again to part of the lecture. Then answer the question.

What does the speaker mean when she says this:

Ⓐ She is reluctant to talk about it.

Ⓑ She doesn't have enough time to talk about it.

Ⓒ She will talk more about it later.

Ⓓ She is unsure about the information.

Q5. Why is it important for the destination countries to know the trend of immigration?

Ⓐ To control their borders

Ⓑ To plan policies accordingly

Ⓒ To inform people in the communities

Ⓓ To be part of globalization

• abroad	**adv**	overseas; out of the country
• migration	**n**	moving from one place to another especially in order to find work or to live
• destination	**n**	the place to which one is going or directed; journey's end; stop; station
• demographic	**adj**	relating to or concerning the study of the characteristics of human population
• pension	**n**	allowance; benefit

Test 2

Q1. What is the main topic of the lecture?

Ⓐ A form of farming system
Ⓑ Discrimination against the black slaves
Ⓒ Benefits of sharecropping
Ⓓ Land policies in the United States

Q2. What does the speaker imply about sharecropping?

Ⓐ It only worked in the ancient times.
Ⓑ It took a long time to settle as a system.
Ⓒ It didn't always benefit the sharecroppers.
Ⓓ It eventually freed black slaves after the Civil War.

Q3. What does the speaker mean when he says this:

Ⓐ He doesn't have anything more to say.
Ⓑ He is not interested in it.
Ⓒ He thinks the point is quite clear.
Ⓓ He finds it difficult to discuss.

Q4. What are the sharecroppers expected to do?

Click on 2 answers.

Ⓐ Do all the work to harvest crops
Ⓑ Share the work with the landowner
Ⓒ Buy off the land from the owner
Ⓓ Take a certain portion of the harvest

Q5. Why couldn't the freed black slaves buy their own cotton fields?

Click on 2 answers.

Ⓐ White landowners wouldn't sell the land to them.
Ⓑ They didn't want to give up sharecropping.
Ⓒ They were unable to save enough money.
Ⓓ Black people were not allowed to own the land.

• harvest	**n**	the gathering of a crop; produce; yield
• plow	**v**	to turn over the soil using a farming tool called a plow
• weed	**v**	to remove weeds from field or garden
• needless	**adj**	unnecessary; without any use; pointless
• wage	**n**	amount of money paid regularly for someone's work
• portion	**n**	section; share; part
• reluctant	**adj**	unwilling; hesitant; unenthusiastic
• in debt		owing someone money or a favor

Nature and Society

Test 3 🔊 54_U5_T3.mp3

Q1. Why does the man come to the office?
- Ⓐ To cancel his registration for a trip
- Ⓑ To register for a field trip
- Ⓒ To get help for his art course
- Ⓓ To look at his school record

Q2. Why does the man have a problem signing up for the field trip?
- Ⓐ He didn't cancel his last trip.
- Ⓑ He can't access the website.
- Ⓒ He didn't go on the last trip.
- Ⓓ He is not a registered student.

Q3. Why didn't the man go on his last field trip?
- Ⓐ He had to go to a soccer game.
- Ⓑ He was busy finishing his final report.
- Ⓒ He couldn't sign up for it.
- Ⓓ He hurt himself playing sports.

Q4. Listen again to part of the conversation. Then answer the question.
Why does the man say this:
- Ⓐ To express his frustration
- Ⓑ To complain about the woman's attitude
- Ⓒ To tell her the truth about something
- Ⓓ To explain his injury

- injure   **v** to hurt; damage; wound
- in bad shape   not in good (physical or situational) condition
- try one's luck   **idiom** to see if things will work out as one desires
- fill in   to substitute; replace; take the place of
- one's best shot one's best effort; the best one can do

Listening Helper 🔊 55_U5_LH.mp3

A. Listen to each sentence and fill in the blank with the correct word(s) you hear. 🎧

1. The evidence of our genetic evolution includes our _____ vision.
2. The _____ of wild animals brought many changes to human culture.
3. The lack of _____ service is quite critical for people living in poor areas.
4. The students should read the campaign posters for each _____.
5. A high unemployment rate will _____ the world's economy.
6. The discovery of fire _____ the first great leap forward in human history.
7. Most international _____ goes to a few wealthy countries.
8. Policy makers need to have a good picture of future _____ changes.
9. Most landowners were _____ to sell the land to their sharecroppers.
10. Mr. Brown _____ himself while he was coaching the basketball team.

B. First, listen to each sentence to complete the blank with the correct word(s). Then choose the word that has the same meaning as the word from the recording. 🎧

1. There is a growing concern about the supply of fresh water _____.
   Ⓐ completely   Ⓑ globally   Ⓒ totally

2. Grant is not really _____ politics.
   Ⓐ interested in   Ⓑ good at   Ⓒ involved in

3. The professor will _____ you _____ the details later.
   Ⓐ raise up   Ⓑ get rid of   Ⓒ inform about

4. Some anthropologists _____ the time which people first began farming differently.
   Ⓐ calculate   Ⓑ value   Ⓒ record

5. We should try to adapt to _____ energy sources.
   Ⓐ optional   Ⓑ different   Ⓒ selective

6. The students need to _____ that no books are allowed during the test.
   Ⓐ remember   Ⓑ analyze   Ⓒ reserve

7. Tom rarely _____ for his classes and he still gets good grades.
   Ⓐ displays   Ⓑ appears   Ⓒ reveals

8. It is _____ that many sharecroppers were unhappy about the system.
   Ⓐ clear   Ⓑ necessary   Ⓒ tedious

9. Cindy was _____ after her swim meet.
   Ⓐ sick   Ⓑ disappointed   Ⓒ upset

10. A large _____ of the harvested crop went to the landowner.
    Ⓐ price   Ⓑ share   Ⓒ benefit

Nature and Society

UNIT 06

Academic Lectures: Arts and Culture
Conversations

•• Target iBT TOEFL Questions

Academic lectures

What is the speaker's attitude when he says this?
What can be said about the speaker when she says this?
What is the speaker's attitude toward…?
Listen again to part of the lecture. What does the speaker mean when she says this?

Conversations

What is the student's attitude when she says this?
Listen again to part of the conversation. What can be said about the librarian?

Practices

Warm Up 🔊 56_U6_WU.mp3

Use the picture and the vocabulary from the box below to fill in the blanks in each sentence. Then listen to the recording to check your answers.

1. Ragtime jazz first began as _____ music in the late 19th century.

2. Isadora Duncan included skipping, running and _____ in her dance _____.

3. A thatched roof was quite _____ among the _____ in 17th century America.

4. Impressionists painted a great deal of _____ scenes.

5. Planning and _____ of buildings used to be oriented according to the _____ environment.

6. During a _____ in medieval times, the _____ was served in a huge fancy container.

| jumping | common | natural | outdoor | dance |
| movements | colonists | construction | feast | salt |

Part I

Practice 1

A Listen to part of a lecture in a music class. Pay attention to the attitude of the speaker and answer the question.

Q. What can be said about the speaker and ragtime jazz when he says this:

Ⓐ He takes it personally.
Ⓑ He finds it boring.
Ⓒ He really enjoys it.
Ⓓ He always listens to it.

B Listen again and fill in the blanks.

Prof(M): Many experts in music would _____ 'ragtime', or 'ragtime jazz' to be _____ American classic music. Ragtime is _____ an originally American music genre even though part of it _____ the rhythms of African music. Ragtime first began in the late 19th century as dance music in _____ in cities like St. Louis and New Orleans. The popularity of ragtime reached its peak between 1897 and 1918, then it began to _____. Now, the most _____ feature of ragtime is its syncopated, or 'ragged' rhythm. This essentially means that weak beats are _____ instead of strong beats. Personally, I can listen to it for _____. By the way, this syncopated beat enabled ragtime to be _____ an American equivalent of minuets by Mozart or... Waltzes by Brahms. Interestingly, this true American classic also _____ a few European classical composers like... Igor Stravinsky and Claude Debussy.

• expert	**n**	a person with a high degree of skill in or knowledge of a subject
• classify	**v**	to organize according to category
• genre	**n**	a particular type of literature, painting, music, or other art form
• rooted	**adj**	based; embedded; ingrained
• slum	**n**	an area of a city where living conditions are very bad; ghetto; hovel
• peak	**n**	high point; climax; summit; top
• die down		to become less intense

Arts and Culture

Practice 2 58_U6_P2.mp3

A Listen to part of a lecture in a dance class. Pay attention to the attitude of the speaker and answer the question.

Q. What is the speaker's attitude when she says this:

Ⓐ Excited
Ⓑ Bored
Ⓒ Suspicious
Ⓓ Frustrated

B Listen again and fill in the blanks.

> **Prof(W):** Okay, Isadora Duncan... let's see... where should I begin... I mean, she was a woman of many _____; she was a dancer, an adventurer, a poet, a radical thinker and so _____ _____. However, she is most _____ known as a theorist of dance as well as a talented dancer. As a theorist of dance, she developed free and _____ movements that were considered quite radical _____ _____ _____. These movements were _____ the classical Greek art, folk dances, social dances as well as nature. She also _____ ideas from the new American athleticism and _____ skipping, running, jumping and leaping. As a dancer, she was famous for her _____ costumes and bare feet _____ performances. Her movements were simple _____ deep with a new kind of _____. With her revolutionary ideas and passion, she was able to _____ dance to a high place _____ other forms of art and became a _____ of today's modern dance.

• title	ⓝ a descriptive name
• radical	ⓐⓓⓙ extreme; drastic; completed
• prominent	ⓐⓓⓙ widely known; famous; distinguished
• theorist	ⓝ someone who develops an abstract idea or set of ideas about a particular subject
• incorporate	ⓥ to include; assimilate; integrate
• athleticism	ⓝ someone's fitness and ability to perform well at sports or other physical activities

Practice 3

A Listen to part of a conversation in a library. Pay attention to the attitude of the speakers and answer the question.

Q. What can be said about the woman when she says this:

Ⓐ She's upset about the man's attitude.

Ⓑ She wants to leave the place right away.

Ⓒ She is frustrated with her situation.

Ⓓ She is surprised about something.

B Listen again and fill in the blanks.

> **W:** Hi, I'd like to _____ these books.
>
> **M:** Sure. Uh... you know what? Some of these books are _____ and you _____ us 5 dollars.
>
> **W:** No way! I thought they were all _____ today.
>
> **M:** Well, some are. But these three _____ returned two weeks ago.
>
> **W:** Hmm, well, do I pay the overdue charge here?
>
> **M:** Um, no. You need to go downstairs to the _____ office. They'll _____ it for you.
>
> **W:** Okay. I can't believe I got _____ with the due dates.
>
> **M:** Well, you know, it happens.

• overdue	**adj**	past the deadline
• drop off		to quickly deposit or deliver ↔ pick up
• accounting	**n**	the activity of keeping detailed records of money received and spent
• owe	**v**	to be in debt; be obligated
• mixed up		confused

Part II

 60_U6_P4.mp3

Ⓐ Listen to part of a lecture in an architecture class. Then answer the following questions.

Q1. What does the speaker mainly discuss?

Ⓐ Why thatched roofs are popular again

Ⓑ History of different building materials

Ⓒ Effective ways of making a thatched roof

Ⓓ Features of traditional roofing material

Q2. What is the speaker's attitude toward a thatched roof when she says this:

Ⓐ Supportive

Ⓑ Criticizing

Ⓒ Concerned

Ⓓ Unsure

Q3. Which of the following is mentioned as the benefits of a thatched roof?
Click on 2 answers.

Ⓐ It doesn't bend easily.

Ⓑ It lasts a long time.

Ⓒ It is made of hi-tech material.

Ⓓ It is highly insulative.

• thatched	**adj**	covered with straw or reeds
• skeleton	**n**	framework; outline; structure
• reed	**n**	a tall plant with a strong hollow stem that can be used for making things such as baskets
• straw	**n**	dried yellowish stalks from crops
• roofing	**n**	the work of putting new roofs on houses
• flexible	**adj**	being able to bend easily without breaking
• bend	**v**	to curve; lean; turn
• lifespan	**n**	the period of time in which living organisms are normally expected to live
• insulative	**adj**	serving to insulate; keeping safe

B Listen again and find the correct words from below to complete the summary.

Thatched roof

1. _____ skeleton, covered with reeds or straw

Quite common in the 17th century ➡ 2. _____ by other roofing materials

Not seen these days

Benefits

Strength: 3. _____ material
➡ survive the 4. _____

Long 5. _____ :
average 60, up to 100 yrs

High 6. _____ value:
➡ summer - cool,
winter - warm

- insulative
- wooden
- flexible
- replaced
- wind
- lifespan

 Practice 5   61_U6_P5.mp3

A **Listen to part of a lecture in an art class. Then answer the following questions.**

Q1. What is the main topic of the lecture?

Ⓐ Understanding impressionism

Ⓑ The mistakes made by the impressionists

Ⓒ Misconceptions about artists and art critics

Ⓓ The history of impressionism

Q2. What does the speaker imply when he says this:

Ⓐ More people liked the work of impressionists.

Ⓑ The unkind critics also supported the impressionists.

Ⓒ The friendly critics were not being honest.

Ⓓ Too many people criticized the impressionists.

Q3. What is the speaker's attitude when he says this:

Ⓐ Hesitant

Ⓑ Upset

Ⓒ Certain

Ⓓ Disbelieving

• misconception	**n**	an idea that is not correct; error; misunderstanding
• landscape	**n**	outdoor scenes; scenery
• majority	**n**	greater part; common
• harsh	**adj**	cruel; unkind; severe; rough
• patron	**n**	supporter; benefactor; sponsor
• spawn	**v**	to produce; generate
• multitude	**n**	mass; a great many; a large number
• alter	**v**	to change; modify

B Listen again and find the correct words from below to complete the summary.

Impressionism

1st misconception: outdoor painters

But: - painted a lot of 1. _____
- not all their works were done outdoors

2nd misconception: 2. _____ by critics

But: - more 3. _____ critics than unkind ones

Truth:
- influenced generations of artists, 4. _____ and critics
- 5. _____ many art movements in Modern Art
- 6. _____ art

- spawned
- changed
- viewers
- disliked
- landscapes
- friendly

Practice 6 62_U6_P6.mp3

A Listen to part of a conversation between a student and a librarian. Then answer the following questions.

Q1. Why does the woman come to the library?
- Ⓐ To report the missing material
- Ⓑ To ask for assistance on her report
- Ⓒ To find some material for her report
- Ⓓ To extend the time to view the videos

Q2. What is the man's attitude when he says this:
- Ⓐ Kind
- Ⓑ Annoyed
- Ⓒ Anxious
- Ⓓ Cautious

• available	**adj**	accessible; at hand; ready
• extend	**v**	to lengthen; make longer; add to
• panic	**v**	to become hysterical; lose one's nerve; fear

B Listen again and find the correct words from below to complete the summary.

W:	M:
Looking for video tapes for a 1._____	Three videos
	Can't be 2._____ out of the library
	Use a 3._____ room for two hours
2 hours not 4._____, report 5._____ tomorrow	Can 6._____ for another two hours
Sign out the videos	
Take them to upstairs	

- enough
- viewing
- due
- research
- checked
- extend

Arts and Culture •• 111

Test 1

Q1. What is the main topic of the lecture?

Ⓐ The various elements of traditional buildings
Ⓑ The efficiency of environmentally oriented buildings
Ⓒ The architectural influence of natural environment
Ⓓ Regional differences of medieval buildings

Q2. Listen again to part of the lecture. Then answer the question.

What is the speaker's attitude towards modern architecture?

Ⓐ Dissatisfied
Ⓑ Excited
Ⓒ Amused
Ⓓ Indifferent

Q3. Why does the speaker mention the conference center in England?

Ⓐ As an example of a building not limited by the climate
Ⓑ As an example of medieval architecture
Ⓒ To show how it inspired other buildings in different climates
Ⓓ As an example of environmentally oriented architecture

Q4. Which of the following represents a medieval feature in modern architecture?

　Ⓐ Glass box

　Ⓑ Compressed earth walls

　Ⓒ Natural lighting

　Ⓓ Regional distinction

Q5. What does the speaker imply about the field of architecture in the future?

　Ⓐ More research should be done in medieval technologies.

　Ⓑ Radical changes have to be made to conserve energy.

　Ⓒ Standard glass box buildings will become more efficient.

　Ⓓ Buildings will not be limited by regional climate.

• lighting	**n**	the way a place is lit or the quality of the light in it
• conserve	**v**	to save; reserve
• earth	**n**	soil; clay; dirt
• ventilation	**n**	allowing fresh air to get into a room or building
• cutting-edge		foremost; forefront; highly advanced

Test 2

Q1. What is the main topic of the lecture?
- Ⓐ The nutritional value of medieval food
- Ⓑ The diet of the Europeans in the Middle Ages
- Ⓒ The history of the food trade between India and Europe
- Ⓓ The farming economy in Medieval Europe

Q2. What was the most common diet of the people in Medieval Europe?
- Ⓐ Barley and vegetables
- Ⓑ Wheat and various meats
- Ⓒ Barley and cheese
- Ⓓ Wheat and salt

Q3. What is the woman feeling when she says this:
- Ⓐ Uncertain
- Ⓑ In disbelief
- Ⓒ Indecisive
- Ⓓ Curious

Q4. Which of the following was mentioned as a part of rich people's diet in Medieval Europe?
Click on 2 answers.

Ⓐ Spices
Ⓑ Herbs
Ⓒ Cheese
Ⓓ A variety of meat

Q5. Why does the professor mention the expression "above the salt" to the students?

Ⓐ To explain the proper way to place the spices
Ⓑ To show how salt was used in India
Ⓒ To explain why salt was so expensive
Ⓓ To describe how valuable salt was

• barley	**n**	a grain that is used to make food, beer and whisky
• porridge	**n**	a hot, thick and sticky food made with grain and water or milk
• spice	**n**	a variety of powder made from plants to put in food to add flavor
• feast	**n**	banquet; dinner; buffet
• seated	**adj**	placed; settled

Arts and Culture •• 115

Test 3

Q1. What is the topic of the conversation?
- Ⓐ Getting good deals on food
- Ⓑ Getting a discount for student services
- Ⓒ Benefits of living on campus
- Ⓓ Buying meals on campus

Q2. What is the woman's attitude when she says this:
- Ⓐ Regretful
- Ⓑ Ashamed
- Ⓒ Worried
- Ⓓ Careless

Q3. Why is it a good thing that the woman is a commuter?
- Ⓐ She can get a discount on her meal plan.
- Ⓑ She is allowed to buy meal tickets.
- Ⓒ She can eat a greater number of meals.
- Ⓓ She doesn't have to eat on campus.

Q4. What does the woman decide to do?
- Ⓐ Try buying a meal plan for two weeks
- Ⓑ Reduce the number of meals she eats on campus
- Ⓒ Get tickets for 20 meals
- Ⓓ Try to get housing near campus

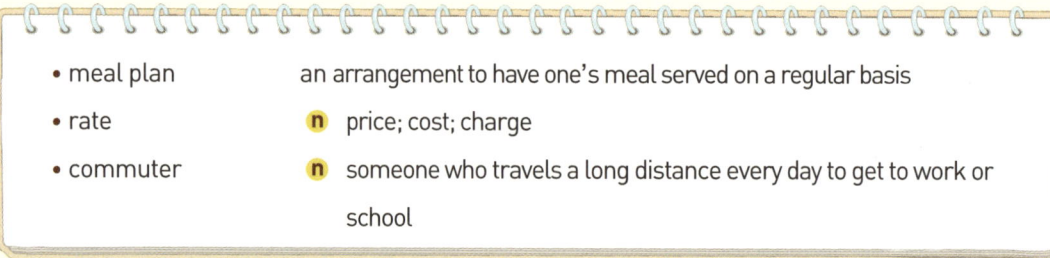

Listening Helper 🔊 66 _U6_LH.mp3

A. Listen to each sentence and fill in the blank with the correct word(s) you hear. 🎧

1. Isadora Duncan is most _____ known as a theorist of dance.
2. These books are at least three weeks _____.
3. To make a thatched roof, the wooden _____ of a roof is covered with reeds or straw.
4. Many people believe that the Impressionists were disliked by the _____ of art critics.
5. Impressionism _____ the way viewers looked at art.
6. Environmentally oriented architecture can _____ up to 80 % of the energy required to build it.
7. People who are getting the award will be _____ in the front row.
8. The rich people sat near the salt during a big _____ in a medieval castle.
9. All _____ are allowed to park their bikes in front of the library.
10. It is important not to _____ during an earthquake.

B. Listen to each sentence to complete the blank with the correct word(s). Choose the word that has the same meaning as the word from the recording. 🎧

1. My father listens to classical music _____ when he is stressed.
   Ⓐ for a few hours   Ⓑ continuously   Ⓒ regularly

2. The technology of compressed _____ walls can conserve a lot of energy.
   Ⓐ planet   Ⓑ globe   Ⓒ clay

3. Part of ragtime jazz is _____ in the rhythms of African music.
   Ⓐ based   Ⓑ unseen   Ⓒ hidden

4. The artist _____ the ideas from the new digital technology.
   Ⓐ integrated   Ⓑ interested   Ⓒ instate

5. My brother asked me to _____ his library books.
   Ⓐ throw   Ⓑ deposit   Ⓒ discard

6. Flexible material can _____ in a strong wind without breaking.
   Ⓐ get together   Ⓑ hold   Ⓒ curve

7. The multitude of art movements were _____ from Impressionism.
   Ⓐ generated   Ⓑ picked up   Ⓒ supported

8. The students asked the teacher to _____ the duration of the test.
   Ⓐ lengthen   Ⓑ spread   Ⓒ pull out

9. The constructors tried to build _____ 21st century green architecture.
   Ⓐ advanced   Ⓑ efficient   Ⓒ complex

10. Jack was happy to get a lower _____ for his subway pass.
    Ⓐ speed   Ⓑ scale   Ⓒ price

Actual Test

Lecture Q.1-5 🔊 67_AT_1.mp3

1. What is the main topic of the discussion?

    Ⓐ American inventors in the late 19th century
    Ⓑ Different types of fencing material
    Ⓒ The development of a popular fencing material
    Ⓓ Problems caused by railroad development

2. Why did the farmers need to use barbed wire fences?
   Click on 2 answers.

    Ⓐ To protect their farms from intruders
    Ⓑ To protest against railroad development
    Ⓒ To keep out roaming animals
    Ⓓ To be able to open their farms more easily

3. The professor and the students discuss several events which happened in the late 19th century America. Put the following events into the correct order.

    | Ⓐ Henry Rose came up with a fencing wire with sharp barbs. |
    | Ⓑ Population increased greatly in the Great Plains. |
    | Ⓒ Barbed wire got mass produced. |
    | Ⓓ Joseph Glidden used two strands of wire to make a fence. |
    | Ⓔ Farmers bought wooden rails to build their fences. |

    ☐ ➔ ☐ ➔ ☐ ➔ ☐ ➔ ☐

4. Which of the following describes the benefits of barbed wire?
   Click on 2 answers.

    Ⓐ Durable
    Ⓑ Heavy
    Ⓒ Natural
    Ⓓ Affordable

5. What does the professor mean when he says this:

    Ⓐ He asks if the students remember the sound of a famous invention.
    Ⓑ He asks if the students have seen one of Glidden's inventions.
    Ⓒ He wants to see if any of the students is named Joseph Glidden.
    Ⓓ He wants to check if the students are familiar with the name.

Lecture Q.6-10 68_AT_2.mp3

6. What is the main topic of the lecture?
  Ⓐ The influence of Dada on World War I
  Ⓑ The relationship between the public and Dada
  Ⓒ An artistic movement against Dada
  Ⓓ The history of Dadaism

7. Why did some artists and intellectuals go to Zurich, Switzerland?
  Ⓐ To meet the Dadaists and see their work
  Ⓑ To get away from the horrors of the war
  Ⓒ To criticize Switzerland's position in the war
  Ⓓ To protest against the Dada movement

8. According to the speaker, what is puzzling about the Dada movement?
  Ⓐ It is not clear where and when it first began.
  Ⓑ It didn't receive any reaction from the public.
  Ⓒ The artists who were part of it denied involvement in the movement.
  Ⓓ It supported the pointless war.

9. What does the speaker imply about the public reaction when he says this:
  Ⓐ The public was excited.
  Ⓑ Only few people showed a reaction.
  Ⓒ It was rather negative.
  Ⓓ It was not very clear.

10. What happened to the Dadaist in the early 1920s?
  Click on 2 answers.
  Ⓐ The public began to reject their ideals.
  Ⓑ Many artists began to support their movement.
  Ⓒ They claimed their work to be non-art.
  Ⓓ They began to disappear from the art world.

Conversation Q.11-14 69_AT_3.mp3

Memo

11. What is the student's problem?

Ⓐ She can't find certain material for her paper.

Ⓑ She needs to change the topic of her research.

Ⓒ She passed the deadline for her paper.

Ⓓ She wants more time to work on her paper.

12. What does the professor suggest to the student?

Ⓐ Share her references with another student

Ⓑ Try to get more interesting references

Ⓒ Find a topic similar to another student

Ⓓ Put more effort into finishing the paper on time

13. What can be inferred about the student when she says this:

Ⓐ She can't find certain material for her paper.

Ⓑ She finished her research too early.

Ⓒ She doesn't need any more material.

Ⓓ She already looked through all her material.

14. What does the professor imply when he says this:

Ⓐ Her paper should be longer than others.

Ⓑ He expects her paper to be good.

Ⓒ She should feel pressured to finish the paper soon.

Ⓓ He feels pressured to give her the extra time.

Lecture Q.15-19 70_AT_4.mp3

15. What is the main topic of the lecture?

- Ⓐ The problems with greenhouse gases
- Ⓑ The importance of eating red meat
- Ⓒ Different types of greenhouse gases
- Ⓓ The effect of red meat on the environment

16. How does the speaker organize his lecture?

- Ⓐ By listing some facts about greenhouse gases
- Ⓑ By giving his opinion about eating red meat
- Ⓒ By illustrating the outcomes of a research project
- Ⓓ By comparing the nutritional value of different types of meat

17. According to the research, why are cows environmentally expensive?

- Ⓐ They produce strong greenhouse gases.
- Ⓑ They have to be transported by automobile.
- Ⓒ They consume more carbon dioxide than chickens.
- Ⓓ They require a lot of gas to digest food.

18. What does the speaker imply about producing food from cows?

- Ⓐ It creates more environmental harm than the automobile.
- Ⓑ It involves heavy uses of automobile.
- Ⓒ It generally consumes less energy than grazing cows.
- Ⓓ Its impact on the environment is still in question.

19. What can be said about the speaker when he says this:

- Ⓐ He is concerned about his health.
- Ⓑ He usually doesn't enjoy red meat.
- Ⓒ He feels the need to change his diet.
- Ⓓ He finds it difficult to eat steaks.

Lecture Q.20-24 71_AT_5.mp3

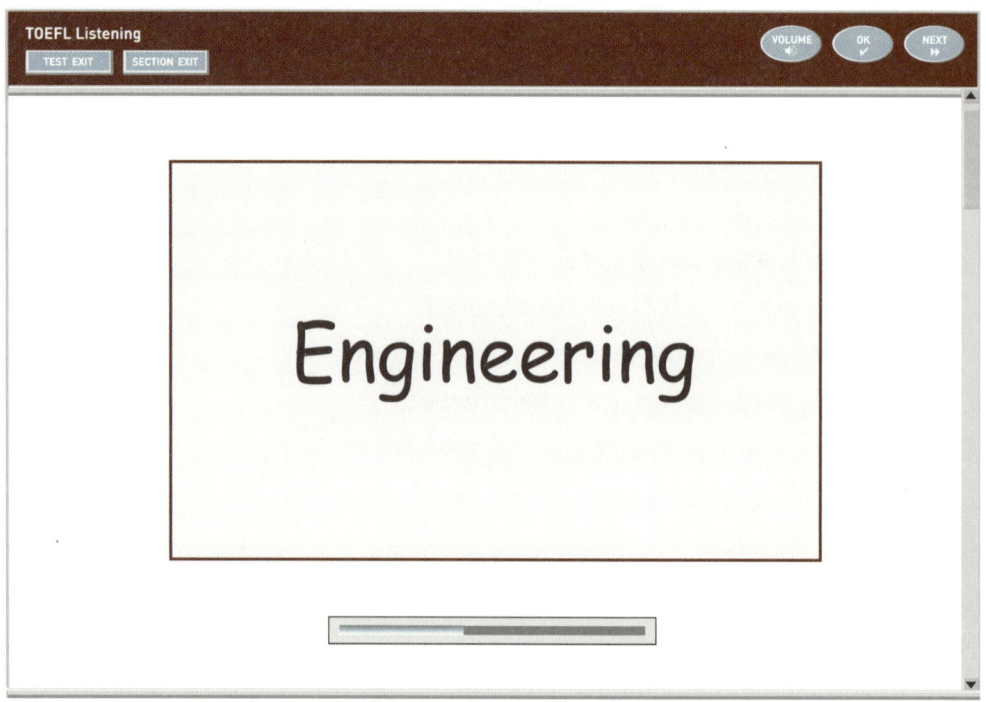

20. What is the main topic of the lecture?
- Ⓐ Installing a device on a special plant
- Ⓑ A plant with animal-like features
- Ⓒ A technology inspired by a plant
- Ⓓ Using a plant for food packaging

21. What causes the mechanical snap of a venus flytrap?
- Ⓐ Muscles
- Ⓑ Temperature
- Ⓒ Humidity
- Ⓓ Cells

22. Which feature of the venus flytrap did scientists try to imitate?
- Ⓐ The sudden snapping
- Ⓑ The killing and ingesting of insects
- Ⓒ The flexible muscles
- Ⓓ The chemical signals

23. Why does the speaker mention food packaging?
- Ⓐ To describe one of the processes the scientists used
- Ⓑ To explain an effective way to store the plant's leaves
- Ⓒ As a way to apply the technology from the venus flytrap
- Ⓓ As a way to trigger the mechanical reaction of the food

24. What can be said about the speaker when she says this:
- Ⓐ She regrets taking a break.
- Ⓑ She feels pressured because of time.
- Ⓒ She has to leave soon.
- Ⓓ She is excited about her talk.

Conversation Q.25-28 72_AT_6.mp3

Memo

25. What is the woman's problem?

　Ⓐ She needs more time to finish the project.

　Ⓑ She is too busy for a group project.

　Ⓒ She wants to switch her project.

　Ⓓ She is unhappy about her group.

26. What can be said about the woman when she says this: 🎧

　Ⓐ She is being careful with her words.

　Ⓑ She doesn't know what to say.

　Ⓒ She is waiting for him to speak first.

　Ⓓ She is feeling pressured to speak.

27. What is the man's attitude toward the woman?

　Ⓐ Frustrated

　Ⓑ Surprised

　Ⓒ Supportive

　Ⓓ Annoyed

28. What does the man imply when he says this: 🎧

　Ⓐ He thinks the woman should leave.

　Ⓑ He is suspicious of her intention.

　Ⓒ He expects her to explain more.

　Ⓓ He wants her to keep things to herself.

Wit&Wisdom iBT TOEFL Series

Beginning (40~60)

The iBT TOEFL Beginner Series

 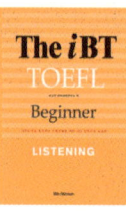  

★
The iBT TOEFL Beginner
Reading / Listening / Speaking / Writing

Perium VOCA Series

★★
Perium VOCA for TOEFL
Reading / Speaking / Writing

The iBT Grammar Series

★★
The iBT Grammar
for Beginners / for All Learners

Wit&Wisdom iBT TOEFL Series

Intermediate (60~90)

The iBT TOEFL Series

★★
The iBT TOEFL
Reading / Listening / Speaking / Writing

The iBT Grammar Series

★★★
The iBT Grammar
Practice Test